EARLY GREEK PHILOSOPHY AND OTHER ESSAYS

EARLY GREEK PHILOSOPHY AND OTHER ESSAYS

FRIEDRICH NIETZSCHE

COPYRIGHT

CONTENTS

THE GREEK STATE

We moderns have an advantage over the Greeks in two ideas, which are given as it were as a compensation to a world behaving thoroughly slavishly and yet at the same time anxiously eschewing the word "slave:" we talk of the "dignity of man" and of the "dignity of labour." Everybody worries in order miserably to perpetuate a miserable existence; this awful need compels him to consuming labour; man (or, more exactly, the human intellect) seduced by the "Will" now occasionally marvels at labour as something dignified. However in order that labour might have a claim on titles of honour, it would be necessary above all, that Existence itself, to which labour after all is only a painful means, should have more dignity and value than it appears to have had, up to the present, to serious philosophies and religions. What else may we find in the labour-need of all the millions but the impulse to exist at any price, the same all-powerful impulse by which stunted plants stretch their roots through earthless rocks!

Out of this awful struggle for existence only individuals can emerge, and they are at once occupied with the noble phantoms of artistic culture, lest they should arrive at practical pessimism, which Nature abhors as her exact opposite. In the modern world, which, compared with the Greek, usually produces only abnormalities and centaurs, in which the individual, like that fabulous creature in the beginning of the Horatian Art of Poetry, is jumbled together out of pieces, here in the modern world in one and the same man the greed of the struggle for existence and the need for art show themselves at the same time: out of this unnatural amalgamation has originated the dilemma, to excuse and to consecrate that first greed before this need for art. Therefore; we believe in the "Dignity of man" and the "Dignity of labour."

The Greeks did not require such conceptual hallucinations, for among them the idea that labour is a disgrace is expressed with startling frankness; and another piece of wisdom, more hidden and less articulate, but everywhere alive, added that the human thing also was an ignominious and piteous nothing and the "dream of a shadow." Labour is a disgrace, because existence has no value in itself; but even though this very existence in the alluring embellishment of artistic illusions shines forth and really seems to have a value in itself, then that proposition is still valid that labour is a disgrace—a disgrace indeed by the fact that it is impossible for man, fighting for the continuance of bare existence, to become an artist. In modern times it is not the art-needing man but the slave who determines the general conceptions, the slave who according to his nature must give deceptive names to all conditions in order to be able to live. Such phantoms as the dignity of man, the dignity of labour, are the needy products of slavedom hiding itself from itself. Woeful time, in which the slave requires such conceptions, in which he is incited to think about and beyond himself! Cursed seducers, who have destroyed the slave's state of innocence by the fruit of the tree of knowledge! Now the slave must vainly scrape through from one day to another with transparent lies recognizable to every one of deeper insight, such as the alleged "equal rights of all" or the so-called "fundamental rights of man," of man as such, or the "dignity of labour." Indeed he is not to understand at what stage and at what height dignity can first be mentioned—namely, at the point, where the individual goes wholly beyond himself and no longer has to work and to produce in order to preserve his individual existence.

And even on this height of "labour" the Greek at times is overcome by a feeling, that looks like shame. In one place Plutarch with earlier Greek instinct says that no nobly born youth on beholding the Zeus in Pisa would have the desire to become himself a Phidias, or on seeing the

Hera in Argos, to become himself a Polyklet; and just as little would he wish to be Anacreon, Philetas or Archilochus, however much he might revel in their poetry. To the Greek the work of the artist falls just as much under the undignified conception of labour as any ignoble craft. But if the compelling force of the artistic impulse operates in him, then he must produce and submit himself to that need of labour. And as a father admires the beauty and the gift of his child but thinks of the act of procreation with shamefaced dislike, so it was with the Greek. The joyful astonishment at the beautiful has not blinded him as to its origin which appeared to him, like all "Becoming" in nature, to be a powerful necessity, a forcing of itself into existence. That feeling by which the process of procreation is considered as something shamefacedly to be hidden, although by it man serves a higher purpose than his individual preservation, the same feeling veiled also the origin of the great works of art, in spite of the fact that through them a higher form of existence is inaugurated, just as through that other act comes a new generation. The feeling of shame seems therefore to occur where man is merely a tool of manifestations of will infinitely greater than he is permitted to consider himself in the isolated shape of the individual.

Now we have the general idea to which are to be subordinated the feelings which the Greek had with regard to labour and slavery. Both were considered by them as a necessary disgrace, of which one feels ashamed, as a disgrace and as a necessity at the same time. In this feeling of shame is hidden the unconscious discernment that the real aim needs those conditional factors, but that in that need lies the fearful and beast-of-prey-like quality of the Sphinx Nature, who in the glorification of the artistically free culture-life so beautifully stretches forth her virgin-body. Culture, which is chiefly a real need for art, rests upon a terrible basis: the latter however makes itself known in the twilight sensation of shame. In order that there may be a broad, deep, and fruitful soil for the development of art, the enormous majority must, in the service of a minority, be slavishly subjected to life's struggle, to a greater degree than their own wants necessitate. At their cost, through the surplus of their labour, that privileged class is to be relieved from the struggle for existence, in order to create and to satisfy a new world of want.

Accordingly we must accept this cruel sounding truth, that slavery is of the essence of Culture; a truth of course, which leaves no doubt as to the absolute value of Existence. This truth is the vulture, that gnaws at the liver of the Promethean promoter of Culture. The misery of toiling men must still increase in order to make the production of the world of art possible to a small number of Olympian men. Here is to be found the source of that secret wrath nourished by Communists and Socialists of all times, and also by their feebler descendants, the white race of the "Liberals," not only against the arts, but also against classical antiquity. If Culture really rested upon the will of a people, if here inexorable powers did not rule, powers which are law and barrier to the individual, then the contempt for Culture, the glorification of a "poorness in spirit," the iconoclastic annihilation of artistic claims would be more than an insurrection of the suppressed masses against drone-like individuals; it would be the cry of compassion tearing down the walls of Culture; the desire for justice, for the equalization of suffering, would swamp all other ideas. In fact here and there sometimes an exuberant degree of compassion has for a short time opened all the flood gates of Culture-life; a rainbow of compassionate love and of peace appeared with the first radiant rise of Christianity and under it was born Christianity's most beautiful fruit, the gospel according to St John. But there are also instances to show that powerful religions for long periods petrify a given degree of Culture, and cut off with inexorable sickle everything that still grows on strongly and luxuriantly. For it is not to be forgotten that the same cruelty, which we found in the essence of every Culture, lies also in the essence of every powerful religion and in general in the essence of power, which is always evil; so that we shall understand it just as well, when a Culture is shattering, with a cry for liberty or at least justice, a too highly piled bulwark of religious claims. That which in this "sorry scheme" of things will live (i.e., must live), is at the bottom of its nature a reflex of the primal-pain and primal-contradiction, and must therefore strike our eyes—"an organ fashioned for this world and earth"—as an insatiable greed for existence and an eternal self-contradiction, within the form of time, therefore as Becoming. Every moment devours the preceding one, every birth is the death of innumerable beings; begetting, living, murdering, all is one. Therefore we may compare this grand Culture with a blood-stained victor, who in his triumphal procession carries the defeated along as slaves chained to his chariot, slaves whom a beneficent power has so blinded that, almost crushed by the wheels of the chariot, they nevertheless still exclaim: "Dignity of labour!" "Dignity of Man!" The voluptuous Cleopatra-Culture throws ever again the most priceless pearls, the tears of compassion for the misery of slaves, into her golden goblet. Out of the emasculation of modern man has been born the enormous social distress of the present time, not out of the true and deep commiseration for that misery; and if it should be true that the Greeks perished through their slavedom then another fact is much more certain, that we shall perish through the lack of slavery. Slavedom did not appear in any way objectionable, much less abominable, either to early Christianity or to the Germanic race. What an uplifting effect on us has the contemplation of the medieval bondman, with his legal and moral relations,—relations that were inwardly strong and tender,—towards the man of higher rank, with the profound fencing-in of his narrow existence—how uplifting!—and how reproachful!

He who cannot reflect upon the position of affairs in Society without melancholy, who has learnt to conceive of it as the continual painful birth of those privileged Culture-men, in whose service everything else must be devoured—he will no longer be deceived by that false glamour, which the moderns have spread over the origin and meaning of the State. For what can the State mean to us, if not the means by which that social-process described just now is to be fused and to be guaranteed in its unimpeded continuance? Be the sociable instinct in individual man as strong as it may, it is only the iron clamp of the State that constrains the large masses upon one another in such a fashion that a chemical decomposition of Society, with its pyramid-like super-structure, is bound to take place. Whence however originates this sudden power of the State, whose aim lies much beyond the insight and beyond the egoism of the individual? How did the slave, the blind mole of Culture, originate? The Greeks in their instinct relating to the law of nations have betrayed it to us, in an instinct, which even in the ripest fulness of their civilization and humanity never ceased to utter as out of a brazen mouth such words as: "to the victor belongs the vanquished, with wife and child, life and property. Power gives the first right and there is no right, which at bottom is not presumption, usurpation, violence."

Here again we see with what pitiless inflexibility Nature, in order to arrive at Society, forges for herself the cruel tool of the State—namely, that conqueror with the iron hand, who is nothing else than the objectivation of the instinct indicated. By the indefinable greatness and power of such conquerors the spectator feels, that they are only the means of an intention manifesting itself through them and yet hiding itself from them. The weaker forces attach themselves to them with such mysterious speed, and transform themselves so wonderfully, in the sudden swelling of that violent avalanche, under the charm of that creative kernel, into an affinity hitherto not existing, that it seems as if a magic will were emanating from them.

Now when we see how little the vanquished trouble themselves after a short time about the horrible origin of the State, so that history informs us of no class of events worse than the origins of those sudden, violent, bloody and, at least in one point, inexplicable usurpations: when hearts involuntarily go out towards the magic of the growing State with the presentiment of an invisible deep purpose, where the calculating intellect is enabled to see an addition of forces only; when now the State is even contemplated with fervor as the goal and ultimate aim of the sacrifices and duties of the individual: then out of all that speaks the enormous necessity of the State, without which Nature might not succeed in coming, through Society, to her deliverance in semblance, in the mirror of the genius. What discernments does the instinctive pleasure in the State not overcome! One would indeed feel inclined to think that a man who looks into the origin of the State will henceforth seek his salvation at an awful distance from it; and where can one not see the monuments of its origin—devastated lands, destroyed cities, brutalized men, devouring hatred of nations! The State, of ignominiously low birth, for the majority of men a continually flowing source of hardship, at frequently recurring periods the consuming torch of mankind—and yet a word, at which we forget ourselves, a battle cry, which has filled men with enthusiasm for innumerable really heroic deeds, perhaps the highest and most venerable object for the blind and egoistic multitude which only in the tremendous moments of State-life has the strange expression of greatness on its face!

We have, however, to consider the Greeks, with regard to the unique sun-height of their art, as the "political men in themselves," and certainly history knows of no second instance of such an awful unchaining of the political passion, such an unconditional immolation of all other interests in the service of this State-instinct; at the best one might distinguish the men of the Renascence in Italy with a similar title for like reasons and by way of comparison. So overloaded is that passion among the Greeks that it begins ever anew to rage against itself and to strike its teeth into its own flesh. This bloody jealousy of city against city, of party against party, this murderous greed of those little wars, the tiger-like triumph over the corpse of the slain enemy, in short, the incessant renewal of those Trojan scenes of struggle and horror, in the spectacle of which, as a genuine Hellene, Homer stands before us absorbed with delight—whither does this naïve barbarism of the Greek State point? What is its excuse before the tribunal of eternal justice? Proud and calm, the State steps before this tribunal and by the hand it leads the flower of blossoming womanhood: Greek society. For this Helena the State waged those wars—and what grey-bearded judge could here condemn?—

Under this mysterious connection, which we here divine between State and art, political greed and artistic creation, battlefield and work of art, we understand by the State, as already remarked, only the cramp-iron, which compels the Social process; whereas without the State, in the natural bellum omnium contra omnes Society cannot strike root at all on a larger scale and beyond the reach of the family. Now, after States have been established almost everywhere, that bent of the bellum omnium contra omnes concentrates itself from time to time into a terrible gathering of war-clouds and discharges itself as it were in rare but so much the more violent shocks and lightning flashes. But in consequence of the effect of that bellum,—an effect which is turned inwards and compressed,—Society is given time during the intervals to germinate and burst into leaf, in order, as soon as warmer days come, to let the shining blossoms of genius sprout forth.

In face of the political world of the Hellenes, I will not hide those phenomena of the present in which I believe I discern dangerous atrophies of the political sphere equally critical for art and society. If there should exist men, who as it were through birth are placed outside the national- and State-instincts, who consequently have to esteem the State only in so far as they conceive that it coincides with their own interest, then such men will necessarily imagine as the ultimate political aim the most undisturbed collateral existence of great political communities possible, which they might be permitted to pursue their own purposes without restriction. With this idea in their heads they will promote that policy which will offer the greatest security to these purposes; whereas it is unthinkable, that they, against their intentions, guided perhaps by an unconscious instinct, should sacrifice themselves for the State-tendency, unthinkable because they lack that very instinct. All other citizens of the State are in the dark about what Nature intends with her State-instinct within them, and they follow blindly; only those who stand outside this instinct know what they want from the State and what the State is to grant them. Therefore it is almost unavoidable that such men should gain great influence in the State because they are allowed to consider it as a means, whereas all the others under the sway of those unconscious purposes of the State are themselves only means for the fulfilment of the State-purpose. In order now to attain, through the medium of the State, the highest furtherance of their selfish aims, it is above all necessary, that the State be wholly freed from those awfully incalculable war-convulsions so that it may be used rationally; and thereby they strive with all their might for a condition of things in which war is an impossibility. For that purpose the thing to do is first to curtail and to enfeeble the political separatisms and factions and through the establishment of large equipoised State-bodies and the mutual safeguarding of them to make the successful result of an aggressive war and consequently war itself the greatest improbability; as on the other hand they will endeavor to wrest the question of war and peace from the decision of individual lords, in order to be able rather to appeal to the egoism of the masses or their representatives; for which purpose they again need slowly to dissolve the monarchic instincts of the nations. This purpose they attain best through the most general promulgation of the liberal optimistic view of the world, which has its roots in the doctrines of French Rationalism and the French Revolution, i.e., in a wholly un-Germanic, genuinely neo-Latin shallow and unmetaphysical philosophy. I cannot help seeing in the prevailing international movements of the present day, and the simultaneous promulgation of universal suffrage, the effects of the fear of war above everything else, yea I behold behind these movements, those truly international homeless money-hermits, as the really alarmed, who, with their natural lack of the State-instinct, have learnt to abuse politics as a means of the Exchange, and State and Society as an apparatus for their own enrichment. Against the deviation of the State-tendency into a money-tendency, to be feared from this side, the only remedy is war and once again war, in the emotions of which this at least becomes obvious, that the State is not founded upon the fear of the war-demon, as a protective institution for egoistic individuals, but in love to fatherland and prince, it produces an ethical impulse, indicative of a much higher destiny. If I therefore designate as a dangerous and characteristic sign of the present political situation the application of revolutionary thought in the service of a selfish State-less money-aristocracy, if at the same time I conceive of the enormous dissemination of liberal optimism as the result of modern financial affairs fallen into strange hands, and if I imagine all evils of social conditions together with the necessary decay of the arts to have either germinated from that root or grown together with it, one will have to pardon my occasionally chanting a Paean on war. Horribly clangs its silvery bow; and although it comes along like the night, war is nevertheless

Apollo, the true divinity for consecrating and purifying the State. First of all, however, as is said in the beginning of the "Iliad," he lets fly his arrow on the mules and dogs. Then he strikes the men themselves, and everywhere pyres break into flames. Be it then pronounced that war is just as much a necessity for the State as the slave is for society, and who can avoid this verdict if he honestly asks himself about the causes of the never-equaled Greek art-perfection?

He who contemplates war and its uniformed possibility, the soldier's profession, with respect to the hitherto described nature of the State, must arrive at the conviction, that through war and in the profession of arms is placed before our eyes an image, or even perhaps the prototype of the State. Here we see as the most general effect of the war-tendency an immediate decomposition and division of the chaotic mass into military castes, out of which rises, pyramid-shaped, on an exceedingly broad base of slaves the edifice of the "martial society." The unconscious purpose of the whole movement constrains every individual under its yoke, and produces also in heterogeneous natures as it were a chemical transformation of their qualities until they are brought into affinity with that purpose. In the highest castes one perceives already a little more of what in this internal process is involved at the bottom, namely the creation of the military genius— with whom we have become acquainted as the original founder of states. In the case of many States, as, for example, in the Lycurgian constitution of Sparta, one can distinctly perceive the impress of that fundamental idea of the State, that of the creation of the military genius. If we now imagine the military primal State in its greatest activity, at its proper "labour," and if we fix our glance upon the whole technique of war, we cannot avoid correcting our notions picked up from everywhere, as to the "dignity of man" and the "dignity of labour" by the question, whether the idea of dignity is applicable also to that labour, which has as its purpose the destruction of the "dignified" man, as well as to the man who is entrusted with that "dignified labour," or whether in this warlike task of the State those mutually contradictory ideas do not neutralize one another. I should like to think the warlike man to be a means of the military genius and his labour again only a tool in the hands of that same genius; and not to him, as absolute man and non-genius, but to him as a means of the genius—whose pleasure also can be to choose his tool's destruction as a mere pawn sacrificed on the strategist's chessboard—is due a degree of dignity, of that dignity namely, to have been deemed worthy of being a means of the genius. But what is shown here in a single instance is valid in the most general sense; every human being, with his total activity, only has dignity in so far as he is a tool of the genius, consciously or unconsciously; from this we may immediately deduce the ethical conclusion, that "man in himself," the absolute man possesses neither dignity, nor rights, nor duties; only as a wholly determined being serving unconscious purposes can man excuse his existence.

Plato's perfect State is according to these considerations certainly something still greater than even the warm-blooded among his admirers believe, not to mention the smiling mien of superiority with which our "historically" educated refuse such a fruit of antiquity. The proper aim of the State, the Olympian existence and ever-renewed procreation and preparation of the genius,—compared with which all other things are only tools, expedients and factors towards realization—is here discovered with a poetic intuition and painted with firmness. Plato saw through the awfully devastated Herma of the then-existing State-life and perceived even then something divine in its interior. He believed that one might be able to take out this divine image and that the grim and barbarically distorted outside and shell did not belong to the essence of the State: the whole fervor and sublimity of his political passion threw itself upon this belief, upon that desire—and in the flames of this fire he perished. That in his perfect State he did not place at the head the genius in its general meaning, but only the genius of wisdom and of knowledge, that he altogether excluded the inspired artist from his State, that was a rigid consequence of the Socratic judgment on art, which Plato, struggling against himself, had made his own. This more external, almost incidental gap must not prevent our recognizing in the total conception of the Platonic State the wonderfully great hieroglyph of a profound and eternally to be interpreted esoteric doctrine of the connection between State and Genius. What we believed we could divine of this cryptograph we have said in this preface.

Philosopher Pyrrho of Elis

THE GREEK WOMAN

Just as Plato from disguises and obscurities brought to light the innermost purpose of the State, so also he conceived the chief cause of the position of the Hellenic Woman with regard to the State; in both cases he saw in what existed around him the image of the ideas manifested to him, and of these ideas of course the actual was only a hazy picture and phantasmagoria. He who according to the usual custom considers the position of the Hellenic Woman to be altogether unworthy and repugnant to humanity, must also turn with this reproach against the Platonic conception of this position; for, as it were, the existing forms were only precisely set forth in this latter conception. Here therefore our question repeats itself: should not the nature and the position of the Hellenic Woman have a necessary relation to the goals of the Hellenic Will?

Of course there is one side of the Platonic conception of woman, which stands in abrupt contrast with Hellenic custom: Plato gives to woman a full share in the rights, knowledge and duties of man, and considers woman only as the weaker sex, in that she will not achieve remarkable success in all things, without however disputing this sex's title to all those things. We must not attach more value to; this strange notion than to the expulsion of the artist out of the ideal State; these are side-lines daringly mis-drawn, aberrations as it were of the hand otherwise so sure and of the so calmly contemplating eye which at times under the influence of the deceased master becomes dim and dejected; in this mood he exaggerates the master's paradoxes and in the abundance of his love gives himself satisfaction by very eccentrically intensifying the latter's doctrines even to foolhardiness.

The most significant word however that Plato as a Greek could say on the relation of woman to the State, was that so objectionable demand, that in the perfect State, the Family was to cease. At present let us take no account of his abolishing even marriage, in order to carry out this demand fully, and of his substituting solemn nuptials arranged by order of the State, between the bravest men and the noblest women, for the attainment of beautiful offspring. In that principal proposition however he has indicated most distinctly—indeed too distinctly, offensively distinctly—an important preparatory step of the Hellenic Will towards the procreation of the genius. But in the customs of the Hellenic people the claim of the family on man and child was extremely limited: the man lived in the State, the child grew up for the State and was guided by the hand of the State. The Greek Will took care that the need of culture could not be satisfied in the seclusion of a small circle. From the State the individual has to receive everything in order to return everything to the State. Woman accordingly means to the State, what sleep does to man. In her nature lies the healing power, which replaces that which has been used up, the beneficial rest in which everything immoderate confines itself, the eternal Same, by which the excessive and the surplus regulate themselves. In her the future generation dreams. Woman is more closely related to Nature than man and in all her essentials she remains ever herself. Culture is with her always something external, a something which does not touch the kernel that is eternally faithful to Nature, therefore the culture of woman might well appear to the Athenian as something indifferent, yea—if one only wanted to conjure it up in one's mind, as something ridiculous. He who at once feels himself compelled from that to infer the position of women among the Greeks as unworthy and all too cruel, should not indeed take as his criterion the "culture" of modern woman and her claims, against which it is sufficient just to point out the Olympian women together with Penelope, Antigone, Elektra. Of course it is true that these are ideal figures, but who would be able to create such ideals out of the present world?— Further indeed is to be considered what sons these women have borne, and what women they must have been to have given birth to such sons! The Hellenic woman as mother had to live in obscurity, because the political instinct together with its highest aim demanded it. She had to vegetate like a plant, in the narrow circle, as a symbol of the Epicurean wisdom λάθε βυῶσας. Again, in more recent times, with the complete disintegration of the principle of the State, she had to step in as helper; the family as a makeshift for the State is her work; and in this sense the artistic aim of the State had to abase itself to the level of a domestic art. Thereby it has been brought about, that the passion of love, as the one realm wholly accessible to women, regulates our art to the very core. Similarly, home-education considers itself so to speak as the only natural one and suffers State-education only as a questionable infringement upon the right of home-education: all this is right as far as the modern State only is concerned.—With that the nature of woman withal remains unaltered, but her power is, according to the position which the State takes up with regard to women, a different one. Women have indeed really the power to make good to a certain extent the deficiencies of the State—ever faithful to their nature, which I have compared to sleep. In Greek antiquity they held that position, which the most supreme will of the State assigned to them: for that reason they have been glorified as never since. The goddesses of Greek mythology are their images: the Pythia and the Sibyl, as well as the Socratic Diotima are the priestesses out of whom divine wisdom speaks. Now one understands why the proud resignation of the Spartan woman at the news of her son's death in battle can be no fable. Woman in relation to the State felt herself in her proper position, therefore she had more dignity than woman has ever had since. Plato who through abolishing family and marriage still intensifies the position of woman, feels now so much reverence towards them, that oddly enough he is misled by a subsequent statement of their equality with man, to abolish again the order of rank which is their due: the highest triumph of the woman of antiquity, to have seduced even the wisest!

As long as the State is still in an embryonic condition woman as mother preponderates and determines the grade and the manifestations of Culture: in the same way as woman is destined to complement the disorganized State. What Tacitus says of German women: inesse quin etiam sanctum aliquid et providum putant, nec aut consilia earum aspernantur aut responsa neglegunt, applies on the whole to all nations not yet arrived at the real State. In such stages one feels only the more strongly that which at all times becomes again manifest, that the instincts of woman as the bulwark of the future generation are invincible and that in her care for the preservation of the species Nature speaks out of these instincts very distinctly. How far this divining power reaches is determined, it seems, by the greater or lesser consolidation of the State: in disorderly and more arbitrary conditions, where the whim or the passion of the individual man carries along with itself whole tribes, then woman suddenly comes forward as the warning prophetess. But in Greece too there was a never slumbering care that the terribly overcharged political instinct might splinter into dust and atoms the little political organisms before they attained their goals in any way. Here the Hellenic Will created for itself ever new implements by means of which it spoke, adjusting, moderating, warning: above all it is in the Pythia, that the power of woman to compensate the State manifested itself so clearly, as it has never done since. That a people split up thus into small tribes and municipalities, was yet at bottom whole and was performing the task of its nature within its faction, was assured by that wonderful phenomenon the Pythia and the Delphian oracle: for always, as long as Hellenism created its great works of art, it spoke out of one mouth and as one Pythia. We cannot hold back the portentous discernment that to the Will individuation means much suffering, and that in order to reach those individuals It needs an enormous step-ladder of individuals. It is true our brains reel with the consideration whether the Will in order to arrive at Art, has perhaps effused Itself out into these worlds, stars, bodies, and atoms: at least it ought to become clear to us then, that Art is not necessary for the individuals, but for the Will itself: a sublime outlook at which we shall be permitted to glance once more from another position.

The Debate of Socrates and Aspasia
by Nicolas-André Monsiau.

ON MUSIC AND WORDS

What we here have asserted of the relationship between language and music must be valid too, for equal reasons concerning the relationship of Mime to Music. The Mime too, as the intensified symbolism of man's gestures, is, measured by the eternal significance of music, only a simile, which brings into expression the innermost secret of music but very superficially, namely on the substratum of the passionately moved human body. But if we include language also in the category of bodily symbolism, and compare the drama, according to the canon advanced, with music, then I venture to think, a proposition of Schopenhauer will come into the clearest light, to which reference must be made again later on. "It might be admissible, although a purely musical mind does not demand it, to join and adapt words or even a clearly represented action to the pure language of tones, although the latter, being self-sufficient, needs no help; so that our perceiving and reflecting intellect, which does not like to be quite idle, may meanwhile have light and analogous occupation also. By this concession to the intellect man's attention adheres even more closely to music, by this at the same time, too, is placed underneath that which the tones indicate in their general metaphorless language of the heart, a visible picture, as it were a schema, as an example illustrating a general idea ... indeed such things will even heighten the effect of music." (Schopenhauer, Parerga, II., "On the Metaphysics of the Beautiful and Aesthetics," § 224.) If we disregard the naturalistic external motivation according to which our perceiving and reflecting intellect does not like to be quite idle when listening to music, and attention led by the hand of an obvious action follows better—then the drama in relation to music has been characterized by Schopenhauer for the best reasons as a schema, as an example illustrating a general idea: and when he adds "indeed such things will even heighten the effect of music" then the enormous universality and originality of vocal music, of the connection of tone with metaphor and idea guarantee the correctness of this utterance. The music of every people begins in closest connection with lyricism and long before absolute music can be thought of, the music of a people in that connection passes through the most important stages of development. If we understand this primal lyricism of a people, as indeed we must, to be an imitation of the artistic typifying Nature, then as the original prototype of that union of music and lyricism must be regarded: the duality in the essence of language, already typified by Nature. Now, after discussing the relation of music to metaphor we will fathom deeper this essence of language.

In the multiplicity of languages the fact at once manifests itself, that word and thing do not necessarily coincide with one another completely, but that the word is a symbol. But what does the word symbolize? Most certainly only conceptions, be these now conscious ones or as in the greater number of cases, unconscious; for how should a word-symbol correspond to that innermost nature of which we and the world are images? Only as conceptions we know that kernel, only in its metaphorical expressions are we familiar with it; beyond that point there is nowhere a direct bridge which could lead us to it. The whole life of impulses, too, the play of feelings, sensations, emotions, volitions, is known to us—as I am forced to insert here in opposition to Schopenhauer—after a most rigid self-examination, not according to its essence but merely as conception; and we may well be permitted to say, that even Schopenhauer's "Will" is nothing else but the most general phenomenal form of a Something otherwise absolutely indecipherable. If therefore we must acquiesce in the rigid necessity of getting nowhere beyond the conceptions we can nevertheless again distinguish two main species within their realm. The one species manifest themselves to us as pleasure-and-displeasure-sensations and accompany all other conceptions as a never-lacking fundamental basis. This most general manifestation, out of which and by which alone we understand all Becoming and all Willing and for which we will retain the name "Will" has now too in language its own symbolic sphere: and in truth this sphere is equally fundamental to the language, as that manifestation is fundamental to all other conceptions. All degrees of pleasure and displeasure—expressions of one primal cause unfathomable to us—symbolize themselves in the tone of the speaker: whereas all the other conceptions are indicated by the gesture-symbolism of the speaker. In so far as that primal cause is the same in all men, the tonal subsoil is also the common one, comprehensible beyond the difference of language. Out of it now develops the more arbitrary gesture-symbolism which is not wholly adequate for its basis: and with which begins the diversity of languages, whose multiplicity we are permitted to consider—to use a simile—as a strophic text to that primal melody of the pleasure-and-displeasure-language. The whole realm of the consonantal and vocal we believe we may reckon only under gesture-symbolism: consonants and vowels without that fundamental tone which is necessary above all else, are nothing but positions of the organs of speech, in short, gestures—; as soon as we imagine the word proceeding out of the mouth of man, then first of all the root of the word, and the basis of that gesture-symbolism, the tonal subsoil, the echo of the pleasure-and-displeasure-sensations originate. As our whole corporeality stands in relation to that original phenomenon, the "Will," so the word built out of its consonants and vowels stands in relation to its tonal basis.

This original phenomenon, the "Will," with its scale of pleasure-and-displeasure-sensations attains in the development of music an ever more adequate symbolic expression: and to this historical process the continuous effort of lyric poetry runs parallel, the effort to transcribe music into metaphors: exactly as this double-phenomenon, according to the just completed disquisition, lies typified in language.

He who has followed us into these difficult contemplations readily, attentively, and with some imagination—and with kind indulgence where the expression has been too scanty or too unconditional—will now have the advantage with us, of laying before himself more seriously and answering more deeply than is usually the case some stirring points of controversy of present-day aesthetics and still more of contemporary artists. Let us think now, after all our assumptions, what an undertaking it must be, to set music to a poem; i.e., to illustrate a poem by music, in order to help music thereby to obtain a language of ideas. What a perverted world! A task that appears to my mind like that of a son wanting to create his father! Music can create metaphors out of itself, which will always however be but schemata, instances as it were of her intrinsic general contents. But how should the metaphor, the conception, create music out of itself! Much less could the idea, or, as one has said, the "poetical idea" do this. As certainly as a bridge leads out of the mysterious castle of the musician into the free land of the metaphors—and the lyric poet steps across it—as certainly is it impossible to go the contrary way, although some are said to exist who fancy they have done so. One might people the air with the phantasy of a Raphael, one might see St. Cecilia, as he does, listening enraptured to the harmonies of the choirs of angels—no tone issues from this world apparently lost in music: even if we imagined that that harmony in reality, as by a miracle, began to sound for us, whither would Cecilia, Paul and Magdalena disappear from us, whither even the singing choir of angels! We should at once cease to be Raphael: and as in that picture the earthly instruments lie shattered on the ground, so our painter's vision, defeated by the higher, would fade and die away.—How neverthe-less could the miracle happen? How should the Apollonian world of the eye quite engrossed in contemplation be able to create out of itself the tone, which on the contrary sym-bolizes a sphere which is excluded and conquered just by that very Apollonian absorption in Appearance? The de-light at Appearance cannot raise out of itself the pleasure at Non-appearance; the delight of perceiving is delight only by the fact that nothing reminds us of a sphere in which individuation is broken and abolished. If we have charac-terized at all correctly the Apollonian in opposition to the Dionysian, then the thought which attributes to the met-aphor, the idea, the appearance, in some way the power of producing out of itself the tone, must appear to us strangely wrong. We will not be referred, in order to be re-futed, to the musician who writes music to existing lyric poems; for after all that has been said we shall be com-pelled to assert that the relationship between the lyric poem and its setting must in any case be a different one from that between a father and his child. Then what ex-actly?

Here now we may be met on the ground of a favorite aesthetic notion with the proposition, "It is not the poem which gives birth to the setting but the sentiment created by the poem." I do not agree with that; the more subtle or powerful stirring-up of that pleasure-and-displeasure-subsoil is in the realm of productive art the element which is inartistic in itself; indeed only its total exclusion makes the complete self-absorption and disinterested perception of the artist possible. Here perhaps one might retaliate that I myself just now predicated about the "Will," that in music "Will" came to an ever more adequate symbolic ex-pression. My answer, condensed into an aesthetic axiom, is this: the Will is the object of music but not the origin of it, that is the Will in its very greatest universality, as the most original manifestation, under which is to be under-stood all Becoming. That, which we call feeling, is with regard to this Will already permeated and saturated with conscious and unconscious conceptions and is therefore no longer directly the object of music; it is unthinkable then that these feelings should be able to create music out of themselves. Take for instance the feelings of love, fear and hope: music can no longer do anything with them in a direct way, every one of them is already so filled with conceptions. On the contrary these feelings can serve to symbolize music, as the lyric poet does who translates for himself into the simile-world of feelings that conceptually and metaphorically unapproachable realm of the Will, the proper content and object of music. The lyric poet resembles all those hearers of music who are conscious of an effect of music on their emotions; the distant and removed power of music appeals, with them, to an intermediate realm which gives to them as it were a foretaste, a symbolic preliminary conception of music proper, it appeals to the intermediate realm of the emotions. One might be permitted to say about them, with respect to the Will, the only object of music, that they bear the same relation to this Will, as the analogous morning-dream, according to Schopenhauer's theory, bears to the dream proper. To all those, however, who are unable to get at music except with their emotions, is to be said, that they will ever remain in the entrance-hall, and will never have access to the sanctuary of music: which, as I said, emotion cannot show but only symbolize.

With regard however to the origin of music, I have already explained that that can never lie in the Will, but must rather rest in the lap of that force, which under the form of the "Will" creates out of itself a visionary world: the origin of music lies beyond all individuation, a proposition, which after our discussion on the Dionysian self-evident. At this point I take the liberty of setting forth again comprehensively side by side those decisive propositions which the antithesis of the Dionysian and Apollonian dealt with has compelled us to enunciate:

The "Will," as the most original manifestation, is the object of music: in this sense music can be called imitation of Nature, but of Nature in its most general form.—

The "Will" itself and the feelings—manifestations of the Will already permeated with conceptions—are wholly incapable of creating music out of themselves, just as on the other hand it is utterly denied to music to represent feelings, or to have feelings as its object, while Will is its only object.—

He who carries away feelings as effects of music has within them as it were a symbolic intermediate realm, which can give him a foretaste of music, but excludes him at the same time from her innermost sanctuaries.—

The lyric poet interprets music to himself through the symbolic world of emotions, whereas he himself, in the calm of the Apollonian contemplation, is exempted from those emotions.—

When, therefore, the musician writes a setting to a lyric poem he is moved as musician neither through the images nor through the emotional language in the text; but a musical inspiration coming from quite a different sphere chooses for itself that song-text as allegorical expression. There cannot therefore be any question as to a necessary relation between poem and music; for the two worlds brought here into connection are too strange to one another to enter into more than a superficial alliance; the song-text is just a symbol and stands to music in the same relation as the Egyptian hieroglyph of bravery did to the brave warrior himself. During the highest revelations of music we even feel involuntarily the crudeness of every figurative effort and of every emotion dragged in for purposes of analogy; for example, the last quartets of Beethoven quite put to shame all illustration and the entire realm of empiric reality. The symbol, in face of the god really revealing himself, has no longer any meaning; moreover it appears as an offensive superficiality.

One must not think any the worse of us for considering from this point of view one item so that we may speak about it without reserve, namely the last movement of Beethoven's Ninth Symphony, a movement which is unprecedented and unanalyzable in its charms. To the dithyrambic world-redeeming exultation of this music Schiller's poem "To Joy," is wholly incongruous, yea, like cold moon-light, pales beside that sea of flame. Who would rob me of this sure feeling? Yea, who would be able to dispute that that feeling during the hearing of this music does not find expression in a scream only because we, wholly impotent through music for metaphor and word, already hear nothing at all from Schiller's poem. All that noble sublimity, yea the grandeur of Schiller's verses has, beside the truly naïve-innocent folk-melody of joy, a disturbing, troubling, even crude and offensive effect; only the ever fuller development of the choir's song and the masses of the orchestra preventing us from hearing them, keep from us that sensation of incongruity. What therefore shall we think of that awful aesthetic superstition that Beethoven himself made a solemn statement as to his belief in the limits of absolute music, in that fourth movement of the Ninth Symphony, yea that he as it were with it unlocked the portals of a new art, within which music had been enabled to represent even metaphor and idea and whereby music had been opened to the "conscious mind." And what does Beethoven himself tell us when he has choir-song introduced by a recitative? "Alas friends, let us intonate not these tones but more pleasing and joyous ones!" More pleasing and joyous ones! For that he needed the convincing tone of the human voice, for that he needed the music of innocence in the folk-song. Not the word, but the "more pleasing" sound, not the idea but the most heartfelt joyful tone was chosen by the sublime master in his longing for the most soul-thrilling ensemble of his orchestra. And how could one misunderstand him! Rather may the same be said of this movement as Richard Wagner says of the great

"Missa Solemnis" which he calls "a pure symphonic work of the most genuine Beethoven-spirit" (Beethoven, p. 42). "The voices are treated here quite in the sense of human instruments, in which sense Schopenhauer quite rightly wanted these human voices to be considered; the text underlying them is understood by us in these great Church compositions, not in its conceptual meaning, but it serves in the sense of the musical work of art, merely as material for vocal music and does not stand to our musically determined sensation in a disturbing position simply because it does not incite in us any rational conceptions but, as its ecclesiastical character conditions too, only touches us with the impression of well-known symbolic creeds." Besides I do not doubt that Beethoven, had he written the Tenth Symphony—of which drafts are still extant—would have composed just the Tenth Symphony.

Let us now approach, after these preparations, the discussion of the opera, so as to be able to proceed afterwards from the opera to its counterpart in the Greek tragedy. What we had to observe in the last movement of the Ninth, i.e., on the highest level of modern music-development, viz., that the word-content goes down unheard in the general sea of sound, is nothing isolated and peculiar, but the general and eternally valid norm in the vocal music of all times, the norm which alone is adequate to the origin of lyric song. The man in a state of Dionysian excitement has a listener just as little as the orgiastic crowd, a listener to whom he might have something to communicate, a listener as the epic narrator and generally speaking the Apollonian artist, to be sure, presupposes. It is rather in the nature of the Dionysian art, that it has no consideration for the listener: the inspired servant of Dionysos is, as I said in a former place, understood only by his compeers. But if we now imagine a listener at those endemic outbursts of Dionysian excitement then we shall have to prophesy for him a fate similar to that which Pentheus the discovered eavesdropper suffered, namely, to be torn to pieces by the Maenads. The lyric musician sings "as the bird sings,"[1] alone, out of innermost compulsion; when the listener comes to him with a demand he must become dumb. Therefore it would be altogether unnatural to ask from the lyric musician that one should also understand the text-words of his song, unnatural because here a demand is made by the listener, who has no right at all during the lyric outburst to claim anything. Now with the poetry of the great ancient lyric poets in your hand, put the question honestly to yourself whether they can have even thought of making themselves clear to the mass of the people standing around and listening, clear with their world of metaphors and thoughts; answer this serious question with a look at Pindar and the Aeschylean choir songs. These most daring and obscure intricacies of thought, this whirl of metaphors, ever impetuously reproducing itself, this oracular tone of the whole, which we, without the diversion of music and orchestration, so often cannot penetrate even with the closest attention—was this whole world of miracles transparent as glass to the Greek crowd, yea, a metaphorical-conceptual interpretation of music? And with such mysteries of thought as are to be found in Pindar do you think the wonderful poet could have wished to elucidate the music already strikingly distinct? Should we here not be forced to an insight into the very nature of the lyricist—the artistic man, who to himself must interpret music through the symbolism of metaphors and emotions, but who has nothing to communicate to the listener; an artist who, in complete aloofness, even forgets those who stand eagerly listening near him. And as the lyricist his hymns, so the people sing the folk-song, for themselves, out of in-most impulse, unconcerned whether the word is comprehensible to him who does not join in the song. Let us think of our own experiences in the realm of higher art-music: what did we understand of the text of a Mass of Palestrina, of a Cantata of Bach, of an Oratorio of Händel, if we ourselves perhaps did not join in singing?

Only for him who joins in singing do lyric poetry and vocal music exist; the listener stands before it as before absolute music.

But now the opera begins, according to the clearest testimonies, with the demand of the listener to understand the word.

What? The listener demands? The word is to be understood?

But to bring music into the service of a series of metaphors and conceptions, to use it as a means to an end, to the strengthening and elucidation of such conceptions and metaphors—such a peculiar presumption as is found in the concept of an "opera," reminds me of that ridiculous person who endeavors to lift himself up into the air with his own arms; that which this fool and which the opera according to that idea attempt are absolute impossibilities. That idea of the opera does not demand perhaps an abuse from music but—as I said—an impossibility. Music never can become a means; one may push, screw, torture it; as tone, as roll of the drum, in its crudest and simplest stages, it still defeats poetry and abases the latter to its reflection. The opera as a species of art according to that concept is therefore not only an aberration of music, but an erroneous conception of aesthetics. If I herewith, after all, justify the nature of the opera for aesthetics, I am of course far from justifying at the same time bad opera music or bad opera-verses. The worst music can still mean, as compared with the best poetry, the Dionysian world-subsoil, and the worst poetry can be mirror, image and reflection of this subsoil, if together with the best music: as certainly, namely, as the single tone against the metaphor is already Dionysian, and the single metaphor together with idea and word against music is already Apollonian. Yea, even bad music together with bad poetry can still inform as to the nature of music and poesy.

When therefore Schopenhauer felt Bellini's "Norma," for example, as the fulfilment of tragedy, with regard to that opera's music and poetry, then he, in Dionysian-Apollonian emotion and self-forgetfulness, was quite entitled to do so, because he perceived music and poetry in their most general, as it were, philosophical value, as music and poetry: but with that judgment he showed a poorly educated taste,—for good taste always has historical perspective. To us, who intentionally in this investigation avoid any question of the historic value of an art-phenomenon and endeavor to focus only the phenomenon itself, in its unaltered eternal meaning, and consequently in its highest type, too,—to us the art-species of the "opera" seems to be justified as much as the folk-song, in so far as we find in both that union of the Dionysian and Apollonian and are permitted to assume for the opera—namely for the highest type of the opera—an origin analogous to that of the folk-song. Only in so far as the opera historically known to us has a completely different origin from that of the folk-song do we reject this "opera," which stands in the same relation to that generic notion just defended by us, as the marionette does to a living human being. It is certain, music never can become a means in the service of the text, but must always defeat the text, yet music must become bad when the composer interrupts every Dionysian force rising within himself by an anxious regard for the words and gestures of his marionettes. If the poet of the opera-text has offered him nothing more than the usual schematized figures with their Egyptian regularity, then the freer, more unconditional, more Dionysian is the development of the music; and the more she despises all dramatic requirements, so much the higher will be the value of the opera. In this sense it is true the opera is, at its best, good music, and nothing but music: whereas the jugglery performed at the same time is, as it were, only a fantastic disguise of the orchestra, above all, of the most important instruments the orchestra has: the singers; and from this jugglery the judicious listener turns away laughing. If the mass is diverted by this very jugglery and only permits the music with it, then the mob fares as all those do who value the frame of a good picture higher than the picture itself. Who treats such naïve aberrations with a serious or even pathetic reproach?

But what will the opera mean as "dramatic" music, in its possibly farthest distance from pure music, efficient in itself, and purely Dionysian? Let us imagine a passionate drama full of incidents which carries away the spectator, and which is already sure of success by its plot: what will "dramatic" music be able to add, if it does not take away something? Firstly, it will take away much: for in every moment where for once the Dionysian power of music strikes the listener, the eye is dimmed that sees the action, the eye that became absorbed in the individuals appearing before it: the listener now forgets the drama and becomes alive again to it only when the Dionysian spell over him has been broken. In so far, however, as music makes the listener forget the drama, it is not yet "dramatic" music: but what kind of music is that which is not allowed to exercise any Dionysian power over the listener? And how is it possible? It is possible as purely conventional symbolism, out of which convention has sucked all natural strength: as music which has diminished to symbols of remembrance: and its effect aims at reminding the spectator of something, which at the sight of the drama must not escape him lest he should misunderstand it: as a trumpet signal is an invitation for the horse to trot. Lastly, before the drama commenced and in interludes or during tedious passages, doubtful as to dramatic effect, yea, even in its highest moments, there would still be permitted another species of remembrance-music, no longer purely conventional, namely emotional-music, music, as a stimulant to dull or wearied nerves. I am able to distinguish in the so-called dramatic music these two elements only: a conventional rhetoric and remembrance-music, and a sensational music with an effect essentially physical: and thus it vacillates between the noise of the drum and the signal-horn, like the mood of the warrior who goes into the battle. But now the mind, regaling itself on pure music and educated through comparison, demands a masquerade for those two wrong tendencies of music; "Remembrance" and "Emotion" are to be played, but in good music, which must be in itself enjoyable, yea, valuable; what despair for the dramatic musician, who must mask the big drum by good music, which, however, must nevertheless have no purely musical, but only a stimulating effect! And now comes the great Philistine public nodding its thousand heads and enjoys this "dramatic music" which is ever ashamed of itself, enjoys it to the very last morsel, without perceiving anything of its shame and embarrassment. Rather the public feels its skin agreeably tickled, for indeed homage is being rendered in all forms and ways to the public! To the pleasure-hunting, dull-eyed sensualist, who needs excitement, to the conceited "educated person" who has accustomed himself to good drama and good music as to good food, without after all making much out of it, to the forgetful and absent-minded egoist, who must be led back to the work of art with force and with signal-horns because selfish plans continually pass through his mind aiming at gain or pleasure. Woe-begone dramatic musicians! "Draw near and view your Patrons' faces! The half are coarse, the half are cold." "Why should you rack, poor foolish Bards, for ends like these the gracious Muses?"[2] And that the muses are tormented, even tortured and flayed, these veracious miserable ones do not themselves deny!

We had assumed a passionate drama, carrying away the spectator, which even without music would be sure of its effect. I fear that that in it which is "poetry" and not action proper will stand in relation to true poetry as dramatic music to music in general: it will be remembrance-

and emotional-poetry. Poetry will serve as a means, in order to recall in a conventional fashion feelings and passions, the expression of which has been found by real poets and has become celebrated, yea, normal with them. Further, this poetry will be expected in dangerous moments to assist the proper "action,"—whether a criminalistic horror-story or an exhibition of witchery mad with shifting the scenes,—and to spread a covering veil over the crudeness of the action itself. Shamefully conscious, that the poetry is only masquerade which cannot bear the light of day, such a "dramatic" rime-jingle clamors now for "dramatic" music, as on the other hand again the poetaster of such dramas is met after one-fourth of the way by the dramatic musician with his talent for the drum and the signal-horn and his shyness of genuine music, trusting in itself and self-sufficient. And now they see one another; and these Apollonian and Dionysian caricatures, this par nobile fratrum, embrace one another!

[1] A reference to Goethe's ballad, The Minstrel, st. 5:
"I sing as sings the bird, whose note
The leafy bough is heard on.
The song that falters from my throat
For me is ample guerdon." TR.

[2] A quotation from Goethe's "Faust": Part I., lines 91, 92, and 95, 96.—TR.

Alcibiades Receiving Instruction from Socrates, 1776

HOMER'S CONTEST

When one speaks of "humanity" the notion lies at the bottom, that humanity is that which separates and distinguishes man from Nature. But such a distinction does not in reality exist: the "natural" qualities and the properly called "human" ones have grown up inseparably together. Man in his highest and noblest capacities is Nature and bears in himself her awful twofold character. His abilities generally considered dreadful and inhuman are perhaps indeed the fertile soil, out of which alone can grow forth all humanity in emotions, actions and works.

Thus the Greeks, the most humane men of ancient times, have in themselves a trait of cruelty, of tiger-like pleasure in destruction: a trait, which in the grotesquely magnified image of the Hellene, in Alexander the Great, is very plainly visible, which, however, in their whole history, as well as in their mythology, must terrify us who meet them with the emasculate idea of modern humanity. When Alexander has the feet of Batis, the brave defender of Gaza, bored through, and binds the living body to his chariot in order to drag him about exposed to the scorn of his soldiers, that is a sickening caricature of Achilles, who at night ill-uses Hector's corpse by a similar trailing; but even this trait has for us something offensive, something which inspires horror. It gives us a peep into the abysses of hatred. With the same sensation perhaps we stand before the bloody and insatiable self-laceration of two Greek parties, as for example in the Corcyrean revolution. When the victor, in a fight of the cities, according to the law of warfare, executes the whole male population and sells all the women and children into slavery, we see, in the sanction of such a law, that the Greek deemed it a positive necessity to allow his hatred to break forth unimpeded; in such moments the compressed and swollen feeling relieved itself; the tiger bounded forth, a voluptuous cruelty shone out of his fearful eye. Why had the Greek sculptor to represent again and again war and fights in innumerable repetitions, extended human bodies whose sinews are tightened through hatred or through the recklessness of triumph, fighters wounded and writhing with pain, or the dying with the last rattle in their throat? Why did the whole Greek world exult in the fighting scenes of the "Iliad"? I am afraid, we do not understand them enough in "Greek fashion," and that we should even shudder, if for once we did understand them thus.

But what lies, as the mother-womb of the Hellenic, behind the Homeric world? In the latter, by the extremely artistic definiteness, and the calm and purity of the lines we are already lifted far above the purely material amalgamation: its colors, by an artistic deception, appear lighter, milder, warmer; its men, in this colored, warm illumination, appear better and more sympathetic—but where do we look, if, no longer guided and protected by Homer's hand, we step backwards into the pre-Homeric world? Only into night and horror, into the products of a fancy accustomed to the horrible. What earthly existence is reflected in the loathsome-awful theogonian lore: a life swayed only by the children of the night, strife, amorous desires, deception, age and death. Let us imagine the suffocating atmosphere of Hesiod's poem, still thickened and darkened and without all the mitigations and purifications, which poured over Hellas from Delphi and the numerous seats of the gods! If we mix this thickened Boeotian air with the grim voluptuousness of the Etruscans, then such a reality would extort from us a world of myths within which Uranos, Kronos and Zeus and the struggles of the Titans would appear as a relief. Combat in this brooding atmosphere is salvation and safety; the cruelty of victory is the summit of life's glories. And just as in truth the idea of Greek law has developed from murder and expiation of murder, so also nobler Civilization takes her first wreath of victory from the altar of the expiation of murder. Behind that bloody age stretches a wave-furrow deep into Hellenic history. The names of Orpheus, of Musæus, and their cults indicate to what consequences the uninter-rupted sight of a world of warfare and cruelty led—to the loathing of existence, to the conception of this existence as a punishment to be borne to the end, to the belief in the identity of existence and indebtedness. But these particu-lar conclusions are not specifically Hellenic; through them Greece comes into contact with India and the Orient gen-erally. The Hellenic genius had ready yet another answer to the question: what does a life of fighting and of victory mean? and gives this answer in the whole breadth of Greek history.

In order to understand the latter we must start from the fact that the Greek genius admitted the existing fearful impulse, and deemed it justified; whereas in the Orphic phase of thought was contained the belief that life with such an impulse as its root would not be worth living. Strife and the pleasure of victory were acknowledged; and nothing separates the Greek world more from ours than the coloring, derived hence, of some ethical ideas, e.g., of Eris and of Envy.

When the traveler Pausanius during his wanderings through Greece visited the Helicon, a very old copy of the first didactic poem of the Greeks, "The Works and Days" of Hesiod, was shown to him, inscribed upon plates of lead and severely damaged by time and weather. However he recognized this much, that, unlike the usual copies, it had not at its head that little hymnus on Zeus, but began at once with the declaration: "Two Eris-goddesses are on earth." This is one of the most noteworthy Hellenic thoughts and worthy to be impressed on the new-comer immediately at the entrance-gate of Greek ethics. "One would like to praise the one Eris, just as much as to blame the other, if one uses one's reason. For these two god-desses have quite different dispositions. For the one, the cruel one, furthers the evil war and feud! No mortal likes her, but under the yoke of need one pays honour to the burdensome Eris, according to the decree of the immortals. She, as the elder, gave birth to black night. Zeus the high-ruling one, however, placed the other Eris upon the roots of the earth and among men as a much better one. She urges even the unskilled man to work, and if one who lacks property beholds another who is rich, then he hastens to sow in similar fashion and to plant and to put his house in order; the neighbor vies with the neighbor who strives after fortune. Good is this Eris to men. The potter also has a grudge against the potter, and the carpenter against the carpenter; the beggar envies the beggar, and the singer the singer."

The two last verses which treat of the odium figulinum appear to our scholars to be incomprehensible in this place. According to their judgment the predicates: "grudge" and "envy" fit only the nature of the evil Eris, and for this reason they do not hesitate to designate these verses as spurious or thrown by chance into this place. For that judgment however a system of Ethics other than the Hellenic must have inspired these scholars unawares; for in these verses to the good Eris Aristotle finds no offence. And not only Aristotle but the whole Greek antiquity thinks of spite and envy otherwise than we do and agrees with Hesiod, who first designates as an evil one that Eris who leads men against one another to a hostile war of extermination, and secondly praises another Eris as the good one, who as jealousy, spite, envy, incites men to activity but not to the action of war to the knife but to the action of contest. The Greek is envious and conceives of this quality not as a blemish, but as the effect of a beneficent deity. What a gulf of ethical judgment between us and him? Because he is envious he also feels, with every superfluity of honour, riches, splendor and fortune, the envious eye of a god resting on himself, and he fears this envy; in this case the latter reminds him of the transitoriness of every human lot; he dreads his very happiness and, sacrificing the best of it, he bows before the divine envy. This conception does not perhaps estrange him from his gods; their significance on the contrary is expressed by the thought that with them man in whose soul jealousy is enkindled against every other living being, is never allowed to venture into contest. In the fight of Thamyris with the Muses, of Marsyas with Apollo, in the heart-moving fate of Niobe appears the horrible opposition of the two powers, who must never fight with one another, man and god.

The greater and more sublime however a Greek is, the brighter in him appears the ambitious flame, devouring everybody who runs with him on the same track. Aristotle once made a list of such contests on a large scale; among them is the most striking instance how even a dead person can still incite a living one to consuming jealousy; thus for example Aristotle designates the relation between the Kolophonian Xenophanes and Homer. We do not understand this attack on the national hero of poetry in all its strength, if we do not imagine, as later on also with Plato, the root of this attack to be the ardent desire to step into the place of the overthrown poet and to inherit his fame. Every great Hellene hands on the torch of the contest; at every great virtue a new light is kindled. If the young Themistocles could not sleep at the thought of the laurels of Miltiades so his early awakened bent released itself only in the long emulation with Aristides in that uniquely noteworthy, purely instinctive genius of his political activity, which Thucydides describes. How characteristic are both question and answer, when a notable opponent of Pericles is asked, whether he or Pericles was the better wrestler in the city, and he gives the answer: "Even if I throw him down he denies that he has fallen, attains his purpose and convinces those who saw him fall."

If one wants to see that sentiment unashamed in its naïve expressions, the sentiment as to the necessity of contest lest the State's welfare be threatened, one should think of the original meaning of Ostracism, as for example the Ephesians pronounced it at the banishment of Hermodor. "Among us nobody shall be the best; if however someone is the best, then let him be so elsewhere and among others." Why should not someone be the best? Because with that the contest would fail, and the eternal life-basis of the Hellenic State would be endangered. Later on Ostracism receives quite another position with regard to the contest; it is applied, when the danger becomes obvious that one of the great contesting politicians and party-leaders feels himself urged on in the heat of the conflict towards harmful and destructive measures and dubious coups d'état. The original sense of this peculiar institution however is not that of a safety-valve but that of a stimulant. The all-excelling individual was to be removed in order that the contest of forces might re-awaken, a thought which is hostile to the "exclusiveness" of genius in the modern sense but which assumes that in the natural order of things there are always several geniuses which incite one another to action, as much also as they hold one another within the bounds of moderation. That is the kernel of the Hellenic contest-conception: it abominates autocracy, and fears its dangers; it desires as a preventive against the genius—a second genius.

Every natural gift must develop itself by contest. Thus the Hellenic national pedagogy demands, whereas modern educators fear nothing as much as, the unchaining of the so-called ambition. Here one fears selfishness as the "evil in itself"—with the exception of the Jesuits, who agree with the Ancients and who, possibly, for that reason, are the most efficient educators of our time. They seem to believe that Selfishness, i.e., the individual element is only the most powerful agent but that it obtains its character as "good" and "evil" essentially from the aims towards which it strives. To the Ancients however the aim of the agonistic education was the welfare of the whole, of the civic society.

Every Athenian for instance was to cultivate his Ego in contest, so far that it should be of the highest service to Athens and should do the least harm. It was not unmeasured and immeasurable as modern ambition generally is; the youth thought of the welfare of his native town when he vied with others in running, throwing or singing; it was her glory that he wanted to increase with his own; it was to his town's gods that he dedicated the wreaths which the umpires as a mark of honour set upon his head. Every Greek from childhood felt within himself the burning wish to be in the contest of the towns an instrument for the welfare of his own town; in this his selfishness was kindled into flame, by this his selfishness was bridled and restricted. Therefore the individuals in antiquity were freer, because their aims were nearer and more tangible. Modern man, on the contrary, is everywhere hampered by infinity, like the fleet-footed Achilles in the allegory of the Eleate Zeno: infinity impedes him, he does not even overtake the tortoise.

But as the youths to be educated were brought up struggling against one another, so their educators were in turn in emulation amongst themselves. Distrustfully jealous, the great musical masters, Pindar and Simonides, stepped side by side; in rivalry the sophist, the higher teacher of antiquity meets his fellow-sophist; even the most universal kind of instruction, through the drama, was imparted to the people only under the form of an enormous wrestling of the great musical and dramatic artists. How wonderful! "And even the artist has a grudge against the artist!" And the modern man dislikes in an artist nothing so much as the personal battle-feeling, whereas the Greek recognizes the artist only in such a personal struggle. There where the modern suspects weakness of the work of art, the Hellene seeks the source of his highest strength! That, which by way of example in Plato is of special artistic importance in his dialogues, is usually the result of an emulation with the art of the orators, of the

sophists, of the dramatists of his time, invented deliber-
ately in order that at the end he could say: "Behold, I can
also do what my great rivals can; yea I can do it even better
than they. No Protagoras has composed such beautiful
myths as I, no dramatist such a spirited and fascinating
whole as the Symposion, no orator penned such an ora-
tion as I put up in the Georgias—and now I reject all that
together and condemn all imitative art! Only the contest
made me a poet, a sophist, an orator!" What a problem
unfolds itself there before us, if we ask about the relationship between the contest and the conception of the work
of art!—If on the other hand we remove the contest from
Greek life, then we look at once into the pre-Homeric abyss
of horrible savagery, hatred, and pleasure in destruction.
This phenomenon alas! shows itself frequently when a
great personality was, owing to an enormously brilliant
deed, suddenly withdrawn from the contest and became
hors de concours according to his, and his fellow-citizens'
judgment. Almost without exception the effect is awful;
and if one usually draws from these consequences the
conclusion that the Greek was unable to bear glory and
fortune, one should say more exactly that he was unable
to bear fame without further struggle, and fortune at the
end of the contest. There is no more distinct instance than
the fate of Miltiades. Placed upon a solitary height and
lifted far above every fellow-combatant through his incom-
parable success at Marathon, he feels a low thirsting for
revenge awakened within himself against a citizen of Para,
with whom he had been at enmity long ago. To satisfy his
desire he misuses reputation, the public exchequer and
civic honour and disgraces himself. Conscious of his ill-
success he falls into unworthy machinations. He forms a
clandestine and godless connection with Timo a priestess
of Demeter, and enters at night the sacred temple, from
which every man was excluded. After he has leapt over the
wall and comes ever nearer the shrine of the goddess, the
dreadful horror of a panic-like terror suddenly seizes him;

almost prostrate and unconscious he feels himself driven back and leaping the wall once more, he falls down paralyzed and severely injured. The siege must be raised and a disgraceful death impresses its seal upon a brilliant heroic career, in order to darken it for all posterity. After the battle at Marathon the envy of the celestials has caught him. And this divine envy breaks into flames when it beholds man without rival, without opponent, on the solitary height of glory. He now has beside him only the gods—and therefore he has them against him. These however betray him into a deed of the Hybris, and under it he collapses.

Let us well observe that just as Miltiades perishes so the noblest Greek States perish when they, by merit and fortune, have arrived from the racecourse at the temple of Nike. Athens, which had destroyed the independence of her allies and avenged with severity the rebellions of her subjected foes, Sparta, which after the battle of Ægospotamoi used her preponderance over Hellas in a still harsher and more cruel fashion, both these, as in the case of Miltiades, brought about their ruin through deeds of the Hybris, as a proof that without envy, jealousy, and contesting ambition the Hellenic State like the Hellenic man degenerates. He becomes bad and cruel, thirsting for revenge, and godless; in short, he becomes "pre-Homeric"—and then it needs only a panic in order to bring about his fall and to crush him. Sparta and Athens surrender to Persia, as Themistocles and Alcibiades have done; they betray Hellenism after they have given up the noblest Hellenic fundamental thought, the contest, and Alexander, the coarsened copy and abbreviation of Greek history, now invents the cosmopolitan Hellene, and the so-called "Hellenism."

Homer and His Guide (1874)

by William-Adolphe Bouguereau

THE RELATION OF SCHOPENHAUER'S PHILOSOPHY TO A GERMAN CULTURE

In dear vile Germany culture now lies so decayed in the streets, jealousy of all that is great rules so shamelessly, and the general tumult of those who race for "Fortune" resounds so deafeningly, that one must have a strong faith, almost in the sense of credo quia absurdum est, in order to hope still for a growing Culture, and above all—in opposition to the press with her "public opinion"— to be able to work by public teaching. With violence must those, in whose hearts lies the immortal care for the people, free themselves from all the inrushing impressions of that which is just now actual and valid, and evoke the appearance of reckoning them indifferent things. They must appear so, because they want to think, and because a loathsome sight and a confused noise, perhaps even mixed with the trumpet-flourishes of war-glory, disturb their thinking, and above all, because they want to believe in the German character and because with this faith they would lose their strength. Do not find fault with these believers if they look from their distant aloofness and from the heights towards their Promised Land! They fear those experiences, to which the kindly disposed foreigner surrenders himself, when he lives among the Germans, and must be surprised how little German life corresponds to those great individuals, works and actions, which, in his kind disposition he has learned to revere as the true German character.

Where the German cannot lift himself into the sublime he makes an impression less than the mediocre. Even the celebrated German scholarship, in which a number of the most useful domestic and homely virtues such as faithfulness, self-restriction, industry, moderation, cleanliness appear transposed into a purer atmosphere and, as it were, transfigured, is by no means the result of these virtues; looked at closely, the motive urging to unlimited knowledge appears in Germany much more like a defect, a gap, than an abundance of forces, it looks almost like the consequence of a needy formless atrophied life and even like a flight from the moral narrow-mindedness and malice to which the German without such diversions is subjected, and which also in spite of that scholarship, yea still within scholarship itself, often break forth. As the true virtuosi of philistinism the Germans are at home in narrowness of life, discerning and judging; if any one will carry them above themselves into the sublime, then they make themselves heavy as lead, and as such lead-weights they hang to their truly great men, in order to pull them down out of the ether to the level of their own necessitous indigence.

Perhaps this Philistine homeliness may be only the degeneration of a genuine German virtue—a profound submersion into the detail, the minute, the nearest and into the mysteries of the individual—but this virtue grown moldy is now worse than the most open vice, especially since one has now become conscious, with gladness of the heart, of this quality, even to literary self-glorification. Now the "Educated" among the proverbially so cultured Germans and the "Philistines" among the, as everybody knows, so uncultured Germans shake hands in public and agree with one another concerning the way in which henceforth one will have to write, compose poetry, paint, make music and even philosophize, yea—rule, so as neither to stand too much aloof from the culture of the one, nor to give offence to the "homeliness" of the other. This they call now "The German Culture of our times." Well, it is only necessary to inquire after the characteristic by which that "educated" person is to be recognized; now that we know that his foster-brother, the German Philistine, makes himself known as such to all the world, without bashfulness, as it were, after innocence is lost.

The educated person nowadays is educated above all "historically," by his historic consciousness he saves himself from the sublime in which the Philistine succeeds by his "homeliness." No longer that enthusiasm which history inspires—as Goethe was allowed to suppose—but just the blunting of all enthusiasm is now the goal of these admirers of the nil admirari, when they try to conceive everything historically; to them however we should exclaim: Ye are the fools of all centuries! History will make to you only those confessions, which you are worthy to receive. The world has been at all times full of trivialities and nonentities; to your historic hankering just these and only these unveil themselves. By your thousands you may pounce upon an epoch—you will afterwards hunger as before and be allowed to boast of your sort of starved soundness. Illam ipsam quam iactant sanitatem non firmitate sed iciunio consequuntur. (Dialogus de oratoribus, cap. 25.) History has not thought fit to tell you anything that is essential, but scorning and invisible she stood by your side, slipping into this one's hand some state proceedings, into that one's an ambassadorial report, into another's a date or an etymology or a pragmatic cobweb. Do you really believe yourself able to reckon up history like an addition sum, and do you consider your common intellect and your mathematical education good enough for that? How it must vex you to hear, that others narrate things, out of the best known periods, which you will never conceive, never!

If now to this "education," calling itself historic but destitute of enthusiasm, and to the hostile Philistine activity, foaming with rage against all that is great, is added that third brutal and excited company of those who race after "Fortune"—then that in summa results in such a confused shrieking and such a limb-dislocating turmoil that the thinker with stopped-up ears and blindfolded eyes flees into the most solitary wilderness,—where he may see, what those never will see, where he must hear sounds which rise to him out of all the depths of nature and come down to him from the stars.

Here he confers with the great problems floating towards him, whose voices of course sound just as comfortless-awful, as unhistoric-eternal. The feeble person flees back from their cold breath, and the calculating one runs right through them without perceiving them. They deal worst, however, with the "educated man" who at times bestows great pains upon them. To him these phantoms transform themselves into conceptual cobwebs and hollow sound-figures. Grasping after them he imagines he has philosophy; in order to search for them he climbs about in the so-called history of philosophy—and when at last he has collected and piled up quite a cloud of such abstractions and stereotyped patterns, then it may happen to him that a real thinker crosses his path and—puffs them away.

What a desperate annoyance indeed to meddle with philosophy as an "educated person"! From time to time it is true it appears to him as if the impossible connection of philosophy with that which nowadays gives itself airs as "German Culture" has become possible; some mongrel dallies and ogles between the two spheres and confuses fantasy on this side and on the other. Meanwhile however one piece of advice is to be given to the Germans, if they do not wish to let themselves be confused. They may put to themselves the question about everything that they now call Culture: is this the hoped-for German Culture, so serious and creative, so redeeming for the German mind, so purifying for the German virtues that their only philosopher in this century, Arthur Schopenhauer, should have to espouse its cause?

Here you have the philosopher—now search for the Culture proper to him! And if you are able to divine what kind of culture that would have to be, which would correspond to such a philosopher, then you have, in this divination, already passed sentence on all your culture and on yourselves!

Schopenhauer in 1859

PHILOSOPHY DURING THE TRAGIC AGE OF THE GREEKS

If we know the aims of men who are strangers to us, it is sufficient for us to approve of or condemn them as wholes. Those who stand nearer to us we judge according to the means by which they further their aims; we often disapprove of their aims, but love them for the sake of their means and the style of their volition. Now philosophical systems are absolutely true only to their founders, to all later philosophers they are usually one big mistake, and to feebler minds a sum of mistakes and truths; at any rate if regarded as highest aim they are an error, and in so far reprehensible. Therefore many disapprove of every philosopher, because his aim is not theirs; they are those whom I called "strangers to us." Whoever on the contrary finds any pleasure at all in great men finds pleasure also in such systems, be they ever so erroneous, for they all have in them one point which is irrefutable, a personal touch, and color; one can use them in order to form a picture of the philosopher, just as from a plant growing in a certain place one can form conclusions as to the soil. That mode of life, of viewing human affairs at any rate, has existed once and is therefore possible; the "system" is the growth in this soil or at least a part of this system....

I narrate the history of those philosophers simplified: I shall bring into relief only that point in every system which is a little bit of personality, and belongs to that which is irrefutable, and undiscussable, which history has to preserve: it is a first attempt to regain and recreate those natures by comparison, and to let the polyphony of Greek nature at least resound once again: the task is, to bring to light that which we must always love and revere and of which no later knowledge can rob us: the great man.

LATER PREFACE (Towards the end of 1879)

This attempt to relate the history of the earlier Greek philosophers distinguishes itself from similar attempts by its brevity. This has been accomplished by mentioning but a small number of the doctrines of every philosopher, i.e., by incompleteness. Those doctrines, however, have been selected in which the personal element of the philosopher re-echoes most strongly; whereas a complete enumeration of all possible propositions handed down to us—as is the custom in text-books—merely brings about one thing, the absolute silencing of the personal element. It is through this that those records become so tedious; for in systems which have been refuted it is only this personal element that can still interest us, for this alone is eternally irrefutable. It is possible to shape the picture of a man out of three anecdotes. I endeavor to bring into relief three anecdotes out of every system and abandon the remainder.

1.

There are opponents of philosophy, and one does well to listen to them; especially if they dissuade the distempered heads of Germans from metaphysics and on the other hand preach to them purification through the Physis, as Goethe did, or healing through Music, as Wagner. The physicians of the people condemn philosophy; he, therefore, who wants to justify it, must show to what purpose healthy nations use and have used philosophy. If he can show that, perhaps even the sick people will benefit by learning why philosophy is harmful just to them. There are indeed good instances of a health which can exist without any philosophy or with quite a moderate, almost a toying use of it; thus the Romans at their best period lived without philosophy. But where is to be found the instance of a nation becoming diseased whom philosophy had restored to health? Whenever philosophy showed itself helping, saving, prophylactic, it was with healthy people; it made sick people still more ill. If ever a nation was disintegrated and but loosely connected with the individuals, never has philosophy bound these individuals closer to the whole. If ever an individual was willing to stand aside and plant around himself the hedge of self-sufficiency, philosophy was always ready to isolate him still more and to destroy him through isolation. She is dangerous where she is not in her full right, and it is only the health of a nation but not that of every nation which gives her this right.

Let us now look around for the highest authority as to what constitutes the health of a nation. I he Greeks, as the truly healthy nation, have justified philosophy once for all by having philosophized; and that indeed more than all other nations. They could not even stop at the right time, for still in their withered age they comported themselves as heated notaries of philosophy, although they understood by it only the pious sophistries and the sacrosanct hair-splittings of Christian dogmatics. They themselves have much lessened their merit for barbarian posterity by not being able to stop at the right time, because that posterity in its uninstructed and impetuous youth necessarily became entangled in those artfully woven nets and ropes.

On the contrary, the Greek knew how to begin at the right time, and this lesson, when one ought to begin philosophizing, they teach more distinctly than any other nation. For it should not be begun when trouble comes as perhaps some presume who derive philosophy from moroseness; no, but in good fortune, in mature manhood, out of the midst of the fervent serenity of a brave and victorious man's estate. The fact that the Greeks philosophized at that time throws light on the nature of philosophy and her task as well as on the nature of the Greeks themselves. Had they at that time been such commonsense and precocious experts and gayards as the learned Philistine of our days perhaps imagines, or had their life been only a state of voluptuous soaring, chiming, breathing and feeling, as the unlearned visionary is pleased to assume, then the spring of philosophy would not have come to light among them. At the best there would have come forth a brook soon trickling away in the sand or evaporating into fogs, but never that broad river flowing forth with the proud beat of its waves, the river which we know as Greek Philosophy.

True, it has been eagerly pointed out how much the Greeks could find and learn abroad, in the Orient, and how many different things they may easily have brought from there. Of course an odd spectacle resulted, when certain scholars brought together the alleged masters from the Orient and the possible disciples from Greece, and exhibited Zarathustra near Heraclitus, the Hindus near the Eleates, the Egyptians near Empedocles, or even Anaxagoras among the Jews and Pythagoras among the Chinese. In detail little has been determined; but we should in no way object to the general idea, if people did not burden us with the conclusion that therefore Philosophy had only been imported into Greece and was not indigenous to the soil, yea, that she, as something foreign, had possibly ruined rather than improved the Greek. Nothing is more foolish than to swear by the fact that the Greeks had an aboriginal culture; no, they rather absorbed all the culture flourishing among other nations, and they advanced so far, just because they understood how to hurl the spear further from the very spot where another nation had let it rest. They were admirable in the art of learning productively, and so, like them, we ought to learn from our neighbors, with a view to Life not to pedantic knowledge, using everything learnt as a foothold whence to leap high and still higher than our neighbor. The questions as to the beginning of philosophy are quite negligible, for everywhere in the beginning there is the crude, the unformed, the empty and the ugly; and in all things only the higher stages come into consideration. He who in the place of Greek philosophy prefers to concern himself with that of Egypt and Persia, because the latter are perhaps more "original" and certainly older, proceeds just as ill-advisedly as those who cannot be at ease before they have traced back the Greek mythology, so grand and profound, to such physical trivialities as sun, lightning, weather and fog, as its prime origins, and who fondly imagine they have rediscovered for instance in the restricted worship of the one celestial vault among the other Indo-Germans a purer form of religion than the poly-theistic worship of the Greek had been. The road towards the beginning always leads into barbarism, and he who is concerned with the Greeks ought always to keep in mind the fact that the unsubdued thirst for knowledge in itself always barbarizes just as much as the hatred of knowledge, and that the Greeks have subdued their inherently insatiable thirst for knowledge by their regard for Life, by an ideal need of Life,—since they wished to live immediately that which they learnt. The Greeks also philosophized as men of culture and with the aims of culture, and therefore saved themselves the trouble of inventing once again the elements of philosophy and knowledge out of some autochthonous conceit, and with a will they at once set themselves to fill out, enhance, raise and purify these elements they had taken over in such a way, that only now in a higher sense and in a purer sphere they became inventors. For they discovered the typical philosopher's genius, and the inventions of all posterity have added nothing essential.

Every nation is put to shame if one points out such a wonderfully idealized company of philosophers as that of the early Greek masters, Thales, Anaximander,

Heraclitus, Parmenides, Anaxagoras, Empedocles, Democritus and Socrates. All those men are integral, entire and self-contained,[1] and hewn out of one stone. Severe necessity exists between their thinking and their character. They are not bound by any convention, because at that time no professional class of philosophers and scholars existed. They all stand before us in magnificent solitude as the only ones who then devoted their life exclusively to knowledge. They all possess the virtuous energy of the Ancients, whereby they excel all the later philosophers in finding their own form and in perfecting it by metamorphosis in its most minute details and general aspect. For they were met by no helpful and facilitating fashion. Thus together they form what Schopenhauer, in opposition to the Republic of Scholars, has called a Republic of Geniuses; one giant calls to another across the arid intervals of ages, and, undisturbed by a wanton, noisy race of dwarfs, creeping about beneath them, the sublime intercourse of spirits continues.

Of this sublime intercourse of spirits I have resolved to relate those items which our modern hardness of hearing might perhaps hear and understand; that means certainly the least of all. It seems to me that those old sages from Thales to Socrates have discussed in that intercourse, although in its most general aspect, everything that constitutes for our contemplation the peculiarly Hellenic. In their intercourse, as already in their personalities, they express distinctly the great features of Greek genius of which the whole of Greek history is a shadowy impression, a hazy copy, which consequently speaks less clearly. If we could rightly interpret the total life of the Greek nation, we should ever find reflected only that picture which in her highest geniuses shines with more resplendent colors. Even the first experience of philosophy on Greek soil, the sanction of the Seven Sages is a distinct and unforgettable line in the picture of the Hellenic. Other nations have their Saints, the Greeks have Sages. Rightly it has been said that a nation is characterized not only by her great men but rather by the manner in which she recognizes and honors them. In other ages the philosopher is an accidental solitary wanderer in the most hostile environment, either slinking through or pushing himself through with clenched fists. With the Greek however the philosopher is not accidental; when in the Sixth and Fifth centuries amidst the most frightful dangers and seductions of secularization he appears and as it were steps forth from the cave of Trophonios into the very midst of luxuriance, the discoverers' happiness, the wealth and the sensuousness of the Greek colonies, then we divine that he comes as a noble warner for the same purpose for which in those centuries Tragedy was born and which the Orphic mysteries in their grotesque hieroglyphics give us to understand. The opinion of those philosophers on Life and Existence altogether means so much more than a modern opinion because they had before themselves Life in a luxuriant perfection, and because with them, unlike us, the sense of the thinker was not muddled by the disunion engendered by the wish for freedom, beauty, fulness of life and the love for truth that only asks: What is the good of Life at all? The mission which the philosopher has to discharge within a real Culture, fashioned in a homogeneous style, cannot be clearly conjectured out of our circumstances and experiences for the simple reason that we have no such culture. No, it is only a Culture like the Greek which can answer the question as to that task of the philosopher, only such a Culture can, as I said before, justify philosophy at all; because such a Culture alone knows and can demonstrate why and how the philosopher is not an accidental, chance wanderer driven now hither, now thither. There is a steely necessity which fetters the philosopher to a true Culture: but what if this Culture does not exist? Then the philosopher is an incalculable and therefore terror-inspiring comet, whereas in the favorable case, he shines as the central star in the solar-system of culture. It is for this reason that the Greeks justify the philosopher, because with them he is no comet.

[1] Cf. Napoleon's word about Goethe: "Voilà un homme!"—TR.

2

After such contemplations it will be accepted without offence if I speak of the pre-Platonic philosophers as of a homogeneous company, and devote this paper to them exclusively. Something quite new begins with Plato; or it might be said with equal justice that in comparison with that Republic of Geniuses from Thales to Socrates, the philosophers since Plato lack something essential.

Whoever wants to express himself unfavorably about those older masters may call them one-sided, and their Epigones, with Plato as head, many-sided. Yet it would be more just and unbiassed to conceive of the latter as philosophic hybrid-characters, of the former as the pure types. Plato himself is the first magnificent hybrid-character, and as such finds expression as well in his philosophy as in his personality. In his ideology are united Socratic, Pythagorean, and Heraclitean elements, and for this reason it is no typically pure phenomenon. As man, too, Plato mingles the features of the royally secluded, all-sufficing Heraclitus, of the melancholy-compassionate and legislatory Pythagoras and of the psycho-expert dialectician Socrates. All later philosophers are such hybrid-characters; wherever something one-sided does come into prominence with them as in the case of the Cynics, it is not type but caricature. Much more important however is the fact that they are founders of sects and that the sects founded by them are all institutions in direct opposition to the Hellenic culture and the unity of its style prevailing up to that time. In their way they seek a redemption, but only for the individuals or at the best for groups of friends and disciples closely connected with them. The activity of the older philosophers tends, although they were unconscious of it, towards a cure and purification on a large scale; the mighty course of Greek culture is not to be stopped; awful dangers are to be removed out of the way of its current; the philosopher protects and defends his native country. Now, since Plato, he is in exile and conspires against his fatherland.

It is a real misfortune that so very little of those older philosophic masters has come down to us and that all complete works of theirs are withheld from us. Involuntarily, on account of that loss, we measure them according to wrong standards and allow ourselves to be influenced unfavorably towards them by the mere accidental fact that Plato and Aristotle never lacked appreciators and copyists. Some people presuppose a special providence for books, a fatum libellorum; such a providence however would at any rate be a very malicious one if it deemed it wise to withhold from us the works of Heraclitus, Empedocles' wonderful poem, and the writings of Democritus, whom the ancients put on a par with Plato, whom he even excels as far as ingenuity goes, and as a substitute put into our hand Stoics, Epicureans and Cicero. Probably the most sublime part of Greek thought and its expression in words is lost to us; a fate which will not surprise the man who remembers the misfortunes of Scotus Erigena or of Pascal, and who considers that even in this enlightened century the first edition of Schopenhauer's "The World As Will And Idea" became waste-paper. If somebody will presuppose a special fatalistic power with respect to such things he may do so and say with Goethe: "Let no one complain about and grumble at things vile and mean, they are the real rulers,—however much this be gainsaid!" In particular they are more powerful than the power of truth. Mankind very rarely produces a good book in which with daring freedom is intonated the battle-song of truth, the song of philosophic heroism; and yet whether it is to live a century longer or to crumble and molder into dust and ashes, depends on the most miserable accidents, on the sudden mental eclipse of men's heads, on superstitious convulsions and antipathies, finally on fingers not too fond of writing or even on eroding bookworms and rainy weather. But we will not lament but rather take the advice of the reproving and consolatory words which Hamann addresses to scholars who lament over lost works. "Would not the artist who succeeded in throwing a lentil through the eye of a needle have sufficient, with a bushel of lentils, to practice his acquired skill? One would like to put this question to all scholars who do not know how to use the works of the Ancients any better than that man used his lentils." It might be added in our case that not one more word, anecdote, or date needed to be transmitted to us than has been transmitted, indeed that even much less might have been preserved for us and yet we should have been able to establish the general doctrine that the Greeks justify philosophy.

A time which suffers from the so-called "general education" but has no culture and no unity of style in her life hardly knows what to do with philosophy, even if the latter were proclaimed by the very Genius of Truth in the streets and market-places. She rather remains at such a time the learned monologue of the solitary rambler, the accidental booty of the individual, the hidden closet-secret or the innocuous chatter between academic senility and childhood. Nobody dare venture to fulfil in himself the law of philosophy, nobody lives philosophically, with that simple manly faith which compelled an Ancient, wherever he was, whatever he did, to deport himself as a Stoic, when he had once pledged his faith to the Stoa. All modern philosophizing is limited politically and regulated by the police to learned semblance. Thanks to governments, churches, academies, customs, fashions, and the cowardice of man, it never gets beyond the sigh: "If only!..." or beyond the knowledge: "Once upon a time there was..." Philosophy is without rights; therefore modern man, if he were at all courageous and conscientious, ought to condemn her and perhaps banish her with words similar to those by which Plato banished the tragic poets from his State. Of course there would be left a reply for her, as there remained to those poets against Plato. If one once compelled her to speak out she might say perhaps: "Miserable Nation! Is it my fault if among you I am on the tramp, like a fortune teller through the land, and must hide and disguise myself, as if I were a great sinner and ye my judges? Just look at my sister, Art! It is with her as with me; we have been cast adrift among the Barbarians and no longer know how to save ourselves. Here we are lacking, it is true, every good right; but the judges before whom we find justice judge you also and will tell you: First acquire a culture; then you shall experience what Philosophy can and will do."—

3.

Greek philosophy seems to begin with a preposterous fancy, with the proposition that water is the origin and mother-womb of all things. Is it really necessary to stop there and become serious? Yes, and for three reasons: Firstly, because the proposition does enunciate something about the origin of things; secondly, because it does so without figure and fable; thirdly and lastly, because in it is contained, although only in the chrysalis state, the idea: Everything is one. The first mentioned reason leaves Thales still in the company of religious and superstitious people, the second however takes him out of this company and shows him to us as a natural philosopher, but by virtue of the third, Thales becomes the first Greek philosopher. If he had said: "Out of water earth is evolved," we should only have a scientific hypothesis; a false one, though nevertheless difficult to refute. But he went beyond the scientific. In his presentation of this concept of unity through the hypothesis of water, Thales has not surmounted the low level of the physical discernments of his time, but at the best overleapt them. The deficient and unorganized observations of an empiric nature which Thales had made as to the occurrence and transformations of water, or to be more exact, of the Moist, would not in the least have made possible or even suggested such an immense generalization. That which drove him to this generalization was a metaphysical dogma, which had its origin in a mystic intuition and which together with the ever renewed endeavors to express it better, we find in all philosophies,—the proposition: Everything is one!

How despotically such a faith deals with all empiricism is worthy of note; with Thales especially one can learn how Philosophy has behaved at all times, when she wanted to get beyond the hedges of experience to her magically attracting goal. On light supports she leaps in advance; hope and divination wing her feet. Calculating reason too, clumsily pants after her and seeks better supports in its attempt to reach that alluring goal, at which its divine companion has already arrived. One sees in imagination two wanderers by a wild forest-stream which carries with it rolling stones; the one, light-footed, leaps over it using the stones and swinging himself upon them ever further and further, though they precipitously sink into the depths behind him. The other stands helpless there most of the time; he has first to build a pathway which will bear his heavy, weary step; sometimes that cannot be done and then no god will help him across the stream. What therefore carries philosophical thinking so quickly to its goal? Does it distinguish itself from calculating and measuring thought only by its more rapid flight through large spaces? No, for a strange illogical power wings the foot of philosophical thinking; and this power is Fancy. Lifted by the latter, philosophical thinking leaps from possibility to possibility, and these for the time being are taken as certainties; and now and then even whilst on the wing it gets hold of certainties. An ingenious presentiment shows them to the flier; demonstrable certainties are divined at a distance to be at this point. Especially powerful is the strength of Fancy in the lightning-like seizing and illuminating of similarities; afterwards reflection applies its standards and models and seeks to substitute the similarities by equalities, that which was seen side by side by causalities. But though this should never be possible, even in the case of Thales the indemonstrable philosophizing has yet its value; although all supports are broken when Logic and the rigidity of Empiricism want to get across to the proposition: Everything is water; yet still there is always, after the demolition of the scientific edifice, a remainder, and in this very remainder lies a moving force and as it were the hope of future fertility.

Of course I do not mean that the thought in any restriction or attenuation, or as allegory, still retains some kind of "truth"; as if, for instance, one might imagine the creating artist standing near a waterfall, and seeing in the forms which leap towards him, an artistically prefiguring game of the water with human and animal bodies, masks, plants, rocks, nymphs, griffins, and with all existing types in general, so that to him the proposition: Everything is water, is confirmed. The thought of Thales has rather its value—even after the perception of its indemonstrableness—in the very fact, that it was meant unmythically and unallegorically. The Greeks among whom Thales became so suddenly conspicuous were the anti-type of all realists by only believing essentially in the reality of men and gods, and by contemplating the whole of nature as if it were only a disguise, masquerade and metamorphosis of these god-men. Man was to them the truth, and essence of things; everything else mere phenomenon and deceiving play. For that very reason they experienced incredible difficulty in conceiving of ideas as ideas. Whilst with the moderns the most personal item sublimates itself into abstractions, with them the most abstract notions became personified. Thales, however, said, "Not man but water is the reality of things "; he began to believe in nature, in so far that he at least believed in water. As a mathematician and astronomer he had grown cold towards everything mythical and allegorical, and even if he did not succeed in becoming disillusioned as to the pure abstraction, Everything is one, and although he left off at a physical expression he was nevertheless among the Greeks of his time a surprising rarity. Perhaps the exceedingly conspicuous Orpheans possessed in a still higher degree than he the faculty of conceiving abstractions and of thinking unplastically; only they did not succeed in expressing these abstractions except in the form of the allegory. Also Pherecydes of Syrus who is a contemporary of Thales and akin to him in many physical conceptions hovers with the expression of the latter in that middle region where Allegory is wedded to Mythos, so that he dares, for example, to compare the earth with a winged oak, which hangs in the air with spread pinions and which Zeus bedecks, after the defeat of Kronos, with a magnificent robe of honour, into which with his own hands Zeus embroiders lands, water and rivers. In contrast with such gloomy allegorical philosophizing scarcely to be translated into the realm of the comprehensible, Thales' are the works of a creative master who began to look into Nature's depths without fantastic fabling. If as it is true he used Science and the demonstrable but soon out-leapt them, then this likewise is a typical characteristic of the philosophical genius. The Greek word which designates the Sage belongs etymologically to sapio, I taste, sapiens, the tasting one, sisyphos, the man of the most delicate taste; the peculiar art of the philosopher therefore consists, according to the opinion of the people, in a delicate selective judgment by taste, by discernment, by significant differentiation. He is not prudent, if one calls him prudent, who in his own affairs finds out the good; Aristotle rightly says: "That which Thales and Anaxagoras know, people will call unusual, astounding, difficult, divine but—useless, since human possessions were of no concern to those two." Through thus selecting and precipitating the unusual, astounding, difficult, and divine, Philosophy marks the boundary-lines dividing her from Science in the same way as she does it from Prudence by the emphasizing of the useless. Science without thus selecting, without such delicate taste, pounces upon everything knowable, in the blind covetousness to know all at any price; philosophical thinking however is always on the track of the things worth knowing, on the track of the great and most important discernments. Now the idea of greatness is changeable, as well in the moral as in the aesthetic realm, thus Philosophy begins with a legislation with respect to greatness, she becomes a Nomenclator. "That is great," she says, and therewith she raises man above the blind, untamed covetousness of his thirst for knowledge. By the idea of greatness she assuages this thirst: and it is chiefly by this, that she contemplates the greatest discernment, that of the essence and kernel of things, as attainable and attained. When Thales says, "Everything is water," man is startled up out of his worm-like mauling of and crawling about among the individual sciences; he divines the last solution of things and masters through this divination the common perplexity of the lower grades of knowledge. The philosopher tries to make the total-chord of the universe re-echo within himself and then to project it into ideas outside himself: whilst he is contemplative like the creating artist, sympathetic like the religionist, looking out for ends and causalities like the scientific man, whilst he feels himself swell up to the macrocosm, he still retains the circumspection to contemplate himself coldly as the reflex of the world; he retains that cool-headedness, which the dramatic artist possesses, when he transforms himself into other bodies, speaks out of them, and yet knows how to project this transformation outside himself into written verses. What the verse is to the poet, dialectic thinking is to the philosopher; he snatches at it in order to hold fast his enchantment, in order to petrify it. And just as words and verse to the dramatist are only stammerings in a foreign language, to tell in it what he lived, what he saw, and what he can directly promulgate by gesture and music only, thus the expression of every deep philosophical intuition by means of dialectics and scientific reflection is, it is true, on the one hand the only means to communicate what has been seen, but on the other hand it is a paltry means, and at the bottom a metaphorical, absolutely inexact translation into a different sphere and language. Thus, Thales saw the Unity of the "Existent," and when he wanted to communicate this idea he talked of water.

Thales by Wilhelm Meyer

4

Whilst the general type of the philosopher in the picture of Thales is set off rather hazily, the picture of his great successor already speaks much more distinctly to us. Anaximander of Milet, the first philosophical author of the Ancients, writes in the very way that the typical philosopher will always write as long as he is not alienated from ingenuousness and naïveté by odd claims: in a grand lapidarian style of writing, sentence for sentence ... a witness of a new inspiration, and an expression of the sojourning in sublime contemplations. The thought and its form are milestones on the path towards the highest wisdom. With such a lapidarian emphasis Anaximander once said: "Whence things originated, thither, according to necessity, they must return and perish; for they must pay penalty and be judged for their injustices according to the order of time." Enigmatical utterance of a true pessimist, oracular inscription on the boundary-stone of Greek philosophy, how shall we explain thee?

The only serious moralist of our century in the Parergis (Vol. ii., chap. 12, "Additional Remarks on The Doctrine about the Suffering in the World, Appendix of Corresponding Passages") urges on us a similar contemplation: "The right standard by which to judge every human being is that he really is a being who ought not to exist at all, but who is expiating his existence by manifold forms of suffering and death:—What can one expect from such a being? Are we not all sinners condemned to death? We expiate our birth firstly by our life and secondly by our death." He who in the physiognomy of our universal human lot reads this doctrine and already recognizes the fundamental bad quality of every human life, in the fact that none can stand a very close and careful contemplation—although our time, accustomed to the biographical epidemic, seems to think otherwise and more loftily about the dignity of man; he who, like Schopenhauer, on "the heights of the Indian breezes" has heard the sacred word about the moral value of existence, will be kept with difficulty from making an extremely anthropomorphic metaphor and from generalizing that melancholy doctrine—at first only limited to human life—and applying it by transmission to the general character of all existence. It may not be very logical, it is however at any rate very human and moreover quite in harmony with the philosophical leaping described above, now with Anaximander to consider all Becoming as a punishable emancipation from eternal "Being," as a wrong that is to be atoned for by destruction. Everything that has once come into existence also perishes, whether we think of human life or of water or of heat and cold; everywhere where definite qualities are to be noticed, we are allowed to prophesy the extinction of these qualities—according to the all-embracing proof of experience. Thus, a being that possesses definite qualities and consists of them, can never be the origin and principle of things; the veritable ens, the "Existent," Anaximander concluded, cannot possess any definite qualities, otherwise, like all other things, it would necessarily have originated and perished. In order that Becoming may not cease, the Primordial-being must be indefinite. The immortality and eternity of the Primordial-being lies not in an infiniteness and inexhaustibility— as usually the expounders of Anaximander presuppose— but in this, that it lacks the definite qualities which lead to destruction, for which reason it bears also its name: The Indefinite. The thus labelled Primordial-being is superior to all Becoming and for this very reason it guarantees the eternity and unimpeded course of Becoming. This last unity in that Indefinite, the mother-womb of all things, can, it is true, be designated only negatively by man, as something to which no predicate out of the existing world of Becoming can be allotted, and might be considered a peer to the Kantian "Thing-in-itself."

Of course he who is able to wrangle persistently with others as to what kind of thing that primordial substance

really was, whether perhaps an intermediate thing between air and water, or perhaps between air and fire, has
not understood our philosopher at all; this is likewise to
be said about those, who seriously ask themselves,
whether Anaximander had thought of his primordial substance as a mixture of all existing substances. Rather we
must direct our gaze to the place where we can learn that
Anaximander no longer treated the question of the origin
of the world as purely physical; we must direct our gaze
towards that first stated lapidarian proposition. When on
the contrary he saw a sum of wrongs to be expiated in the
plurality of things that have become, then he, as the first
Greek, with daring grasp caught up the tangle of the most
profound ethical problem. How can anything perish that
has a right to exist? Whence that restless Becoming and
giving-birth, whence that expression of painful distortion
on the face of Nature, whence the never-ending dirge in all
realms of existence? Out of this world of injustice, of au-
dacious apostasy from the primordial-unity of things
Anaximander flees into a metaphysical castle, leaning out
of which he turns his gaze far and wide in order at last,
after a pensive silence, to address to all beings this question: "What is your existence worth? And if it is worth
nothing why are you there? By your guilt, I observe, you
sojourn in this world. You will have to expiate it by death.
Look how your earth fades; the seas decrease and dry up,
the marine-shell on the mountain shows you how much
already they have dried up; fire destroys your world even
now, finally it will end in smoke and ashes. But again and
again such a world of transitoriness will ever build itself
up; who shall redeem you from the curse of Becoming?"

Not every kind of life may have been welcome to a man
who put such questions, whose upward-soaring thinking
continually broke the empiric ropes, in order to take at
once to the highest, superlunary flight. Willingly we believe
tradition, that he walked along in especially dignified attire
and showed a truly tragic hauteur in his gestures and

habits of life. He lived as he wrote; he spoke as solemnly as he dressed himself, he raised his hand and placed his foot as if this existence was a tragedy, and he had been born in order to co-operate in that tragedy by playing the role of hero. In all that he was the great model of Emped-ocles. His fellow-citizens elected him the leader of an emigrating colony—perhaps they were pleased at being able to honour him and at the same time to get rid of him. His thought also emigrated and founded colonies; in Ephe-sus and in Elea they could not get rid of him; and if they could not resolve upon staying at the spot where he stood, they nevertheless knew that they had been led there by him, whence they now prepared to proceed without him.

Thales shows the need of simplifying the empire of plu-rality, and of reducing it to a mere expansion or disguise of the one single existing quality, water. Anaximander goes beyond him with two steps. Firstly, he puts the question to himself: How, if there exists an eternal Unity at all, is that Plurality possible? and he takes the answer out of the contradictory, self-devouring and denying character of this Plurality. The existence of this Plurality becomes a moral phenomenon to him; it is not justified; it expiates itself continually through destruction. But then the ques-tions occur to him: Yet why has not everything that has become perished long ago, since, indeed, quite an eternity of time has already gone by? Whence the ceaseless current of the River of Becoming? He can save himself from these questions only by mystic possibilities: the eternal Becom-ing can have its origin only in the eternal "Being," the conditions for that apostasy from that eternal "Being" to a Becoming in injustice are ever the same, the constellation of things cannot help itself being thus fashioned, that no end is to be seen of that stepping forth of the individual being out of the lap of the "Indefinite." At this Anaximan-der stayed; that is, he remained within the deep shadows which like gigantic specters were lying on the mountain range of such a world-perception. The more one wanted to approach the problem of solving how out of the Indefinite the Definite, out of the Eternal the Temporal, out of the Just the Unjust could by secession ever originate, the darker the night became.——

5

Towards the midst of this mystic night, in which Anaximander's problem of the Becoming was wrapped up, Heraclitus of Ephesus approached and illuminated it by a divine flash of lightning. "I contemplate the Becoming," he exclaimed,—"and nobody has so attentively watched this eternal wave-surging and rhythm of things. And what do I behold? Lawfulness, infallible certainty, ever equal paths of Justice, condemning Erinyes behind all transgressions of the laws, the whole world the spectacle of a governing justice and of demoniacally omnipresent natural forces subject to justice's sway. I do not behold the punishment of that which has become, but the justification of Becoming. When has sacrilege, when has apostasy manifested itself in inviolable forms, in laws esteemed sacred? Where injustice sways, there is caprice, disorder, irregularity, contradiction; where however Law and Zeus' daughter, Dike, rule alone, as in this world, how could the sphere of guilt, of expiation, of judgment, and as it were the place of execution of all condemned ones be there?"

From this intuition Heraclitus took two coherent negations, which are put into the right light only by a comparison with the propositions of his predecessor. Firstly, he denied the duality of two quite diverse worlds, into the assumption of which Anaximander had been pushed; he no longer distinguished a physical world from a metaphysical, a realm of definite qualities from a realm of indefinable indefiniteness. Now after this first step he could neither be kept back any longer from a still greater audacity of denying: he denied "Being" altogether. For this one world which was left to him,—shielded all round by eternal, unwritten laws, flowing up and down in the brazen beat of rhythm,—shows nowhere persistence, indestructibility, a bulwark in the stream. Louder than Anaximander, Heraclitus exclaimed: "I see nothing but Becoming. Be not deceived! It is the fault of your limited outlook and not the fault of the essence of things if you believe that you see firm land anywhere in the ocean of Becoming and Passing. You need names for things, just as if they had a rigid permanence, but the very river in which you bathe a second time is no longer the same one which you entered before."

Heraclitus has as his royal property the highest power of intuitive conception, whereas towards the other mode of conception which is consummated by ideas and logical combinations, that is towards reason, he shows himself cool, apathetic, even hostile, and he seems to derive a pleasure when he is able to contradict reason by means of a truth gained intuitively, and this he does in such propositions as: "Everything has always its opposite within itself," so fearlessly that Aristotle before the tribunal of Reason accuses him of the highest crime, of having sinned against the law of opposition. Intuitive representation however embraces two things: firstly, the present, motley, changing world, pressing on us in all experiences, secondly, the conditions by means of which alone any experience of this world becomes possible: time and space. For these are able to be intuitively apprehended, purely in themselves and independent of any experience; i.e., they can be perceived, although they are without definite contents. If now Heraclitus considered time in this fashion, dissociated from all experiences, he had in it the most instructive monogram of all that which falls within the realm of intuitive conception. Just as he conceived of time, so also for instance did Schopenhauer, who repeatedly says of it: that in it every instant exists only in so far as it has annihilated the preceding one, its father, in order to be itself effaced equally quickly; that past and future are as unreal as any dream; that the present is only the dimensionless and unstable boundary between the two; that however, like time, so space, and again like the latter, so also everything that is simultaneously in space and time, has only a relative existence, only through and for the sake of a something else, of the same kind as itself, i.e., existing only under the same limitations. This truth is in the highest degree self-evident, accessible to everyone, and just for that very reason, abstractly and rationally, it is only attained with great difficulty. Whoever has this truth before his eyes must however also proceed at once to the next Heraclitean consequence and say that the whole essence of actuality is in fact activity, and that for actuality there is no other kind of existence and reality, as Schopenhauer has likewise expounded ("The World As Will And Idea," Vol. I., Bk. I, sec. 4): "Only as active does it fill space and time: its action upon the immediate object determines the perception in which alone it exists: the effect of the action of any material object upon any other, is known only in so far as the latter acts upon the immediate object in a different way from that in which it acted before; it consists in this alone. Cause and effect thus constitute the whole nature of matter; its true being is its action. The totality of everything material is therefore very appropriately called in German Wirklichkeit (actuality)—a word which is far more expressive than Realität (reality).[2] That upon which actuality acts is always matter; actuality's whole 'Being' and essence therefore consist only in the orderly change, which one part of it causes in another, and is therefore wholly relative, according to a relation which is valid only within the boundary of actuality, as in the case of time and space."

The eternal and exclusive Becoming, the total instability of all reality and actuality, which continually works and becomes and never is, as Heraclitus teaches—is an awful and appalling conception, and in its effects most nearly related to that sensation, by which during an earthquake one loses confidence in the firmly-grounded earth. It required an astonishing strength to translate this effect into its opposite, into the sublime, into happy astonishment. Heraclitus accomplished this through an observation of the proper course of all Becoming and Passing, which he conceived of under the form of polarity, as the divergence of a force into two qualitatively different, opposite actions, striving after reunion. A quality is set continually at variance with itself and separates itself into its opposites: these opposites continually strive again one towards another. The common people of course think to recognize something rigid, completed, consistent; but the fact of the matter is that at any instant, bright and dark, sour and sweet are side by side and attached to one another like two wrestlers of whom sometimes the one succeeds, sometimes the other. According to Heraclitus honey is at the same time sweet and bitter, and the world itself an amphora whose contents constantly need stirring up. Out of the war of the opposites all Becoming originates; the definite and to us seemingly persistent qualities express only the momentary predominance of the one fighter, but with that the war is not at an end; the wrestling continues to all eternity. Everything happens according to this struggle, and this very struggle manifests eternal justice. It is a wonderful conception, drawn from the purest source of Hellenism, which considers the struggle as the continual sway of a homogeneous, severe justice bound by eternal laws. Only a Greek was able to consider this conception as the fundament of a Cosmodicy; it is Hesiod's good Eris transfigured into the cosmic principle, it is the idea of a contest, an idea held by individual Greeks and by their State, and translated out of the gymnasia and palæstra, out of the artistic agonistics, out of the struggle of the political parties and of the towns into the most general principle, so that the machinery of the universe is regulated by it. Just as every Greek fought as though he alone were in the right, and as though an absolutely sure standard of judicial opinion could at any instant decide whither victory is inclining, thus the qualities wrestle one with another, according to inviolable laws and standards which are inherent in the struggle. The Things themselves in the permanency of which the limited intellect of man and animal believes, do not "exist" at all; they are as the fierce flashing and fiery sparkling of drawn swords, as the stars of Victory rising with a radiant resplendence in the battle of the opposite qualities.

That struggle which is peculiar to all Becoming, that eternal interchange of victory is again described by Schopenhauer: ("The World As Will And Idea," Vol. I., Bk. 2, sec. 27) "The permanent matter must constantly change its form; for under the guidance of causality, mechanical, physical, chemical, and organic phenomena, eagerly striving to appear, wrest the matter from each other, for each desires to reveal its own Idea. This strife may be followed up through the whole of nature; indeed, nature exists only through it." The following pages give the most noteworthy illustrations of this struggle, only that the prevailing tone of this description ever remains other than that of Heraclitus in so far as to Schopenhauer the struggle is a proof of the Will to Life falling out with itself; it is to him a feasting on itself on the part of this dismal, dull impulse, as a phenomenon on the whole horrible and not at all making for happiness. The arena and the object of this struggle is Matter,—which some natural forces alternately endeavor to disintegrate and build up again at the expense of other natural forces,—as also Space and Time, the union of which through causality is this very matter.

[2] Mira in quibusdam rebus verborum proprietas est, et consuetudo sermonis antiqui quædam efficacissimis notis signat (Seneca, Epist. 81).—TR.

6

Whilst the imagination of Heraclitus measured the restlessly moving universe, the "actuality" (Wirklichkeit), with the eye of the happy spectator, who sees innumerable pairs wrestling in joyous combat entrusted to the superintendence of severe umpires, a still higher presentiment seized him, he no longer could contemplate the wrestling pairs and the umpires, separated one from another; the very umpires seemed to fight, and the fighters seemed to be their own judges—yea, since at the bottom he conceived only of the one Justice eternally swaying, he dared to exclaim: "The contest of The Many is itself pure justice. And after all: The One is The Many. For what are all those qualities according to their nature? Are they immortal gods? Are they separate beings working for themselves from the beginning and without end? And if the world which we see knows only Becoming and Passing but no Permanence, should perhaps those qualities constitute a differently fashioned metaphysical world, true, not a world of unity as Anaximander sought behind the fluttering veil of plurality, but a world of eternal and essential pluralities?" Is it possible that however violently he had denied such duality, Heraclitus has after all by a round-about way accidentally got into the dual cosmic order, an order with an Olympus of numerous immortal gods and demons,— viz., many realities,—and with a human world, which sees only the dust-cloud of the Olympic struggle and the flashing of divine spears,—i.e., only a Becoming? Anaximander had fled just from these definite qualities into the lap of the metaphysical "Indefinite"; because the former became and passed, he had denied them a true and essential existence; however, should it not seem now as if the Becoming is only the looming-into-view of a struggle of eternal qualities? When we speak of the Becoming, should not the original cause of this be sought in the peculiar feebleness of human cognition—whereas in the nature of things there is perhaps no Becoming, but only a co-existing of many true increate indestructible realities?

These are Heraclitean loopholes and labyrinths; he exclaims once again: "The 'One' is the 'Many'." The many perceptible qualities are neither eternal entities, nor phantasmata of our senses (Anaxagoras conceives them later on as the former, Parmenides as the latter), they are neither rigid, sovereign "Being" nor fleeting Appearance hovering in human minds. The third possibility which alone was left to Heraclitus nobody will be able to divine with dialectic sagacity and as it were by calculation, for what he invented here is a rarity even in the realm of mystic incredibilities and unexpected cosmic metaphors.—The world is the Game of Zeus, or expressed more physically, the game of fire with itself, the "One" is only in this sense at the same time the "Many."

In order to elucidate in the first place, the introduction of fire as a world-shaping force, I recall how Anaximander had further developed the theory of water as the origin of things. Placing confidence in the essential part of Thales' theory, and strengthening and adding to the latter's observations, Anaximander however was not to be convinced that before the water and, as it were, after the water there was no further stage of quality: no, to him out of the Warm and the Cold the Moist seemed to form itself, and the Warm and the Cold therefore were supposed to be the preliminary stages, the still more original qualities. With their issuing forth from the primordial existence of the "Indefinite," Becoming begins. Heraclitus who as physicist subordinated himself to the importance of Anaximander, explains to himself this Anaximandrian "Warm" as the respiration, the warm breath, the dry vapors, in short as the fiery element: about this fire he now enunciates the same as Thales and Anaximander had enunciated about the water: that in innumerable metamorphoses it was passing along the path of Becoming, especially in the three chief aggregate stages as something Warm, Moist, and Firm. For water in descending is transformed into earth, in ascending into fire: or as Heraclitus appears to have expressed himself more exactly: from the sea ascend only the pure vapors which serve as food to the divine fire of the stars, from the earth only the dark, foggy ones, from which the Moist derives its nourishment. The pure vapors are the transitional stage in the passing of sea into fire, the impure the transitional stage in the passing of earth into water. Thus, the two paths of metamorphosis of the fire run continuously side by side, upwards and downwards, to and fro, from fire to water, from water to earth, from earth back again to water, from water to fire. Whereas Heraclitus is a follower of Anaximander in the most important of these conceptions, e.g., that the fire is kept up by the evaporations, or herein, that out of the water is dissolved partly earth, partly fire; he is on the other hand quite independent and in opposition to Anaximander in excluding the "Cold" from the physical process, whilst Anaximander had put it side by side with the "Warm" as having the same rights, so as to let the "Moist" originate out of both. To do so, was of course a necessity to Heraclitus, for if everything is to be fire, then, however many possibilities of its transformation might be assumed, nothing can exist that would be the absolute antithesis to fire; he has, therefore, probably interpreted only as a degree of the "Warm" that which is called the "Cold," and he could justify this interpretation without difficulty. Much more important than this deviation from the doctrine of Anaximander is a further agreement; he, like the latter, believes in an end of the world periodically repeating itself and in an ever-renewed emerging of another world out of the all-destroying world-fire. The period during which the world hastens towards that world-fire and the dissolution into pure fire is characterized by him most strikingly as a demand and a need; the state of being completely swallowed up by the fire as satiety; and now to us remains the question as to how he understood and named the newly awakening impulse for world-creation, the pouring-out-of-itself into the forms of plurality. The Greek proverb seems to come to our assistance with the thought that "satiety gives birth to crime" (the Hybris) and one may indeed ask oneself for a minute whether perhaps Heraclitus has derived that return to plurality out of the Hybris. Let us just take this thought seriously: in its light the face of Heraclitus changes before our eyes, the proud gleam of his eyes dies out, a wrinkled expression of painful resignation, of impotence becomes distinct, it seems that we know why later antiquity called him the "weeping philosopher." Is not the whole world-process now an act of punishment of the Hybris? The plurality the result of a crime? The transformation of the pure into the impure, the consequence of injustice? Is not the guilt now shifted into the essence of the things and indeed, the world of Becoming and of individuals accordingly exonerated from guilt; yet at the same time are they not condemned for ever and ever to bear the consequences of guilt?

7

That dangerous word, Hybris, is indeed the touchstone for every Heraclitean; here he may show whether he has understood or mistaken his master. Is there in this world: Guilt, injustice, contradiction, suffering?

Yes, exclaims Heraclitus, but only for the limited human being, who sees divergently and not convergently, not for the contuitive god; to him everything opposing converges into one harmony, invisible it is true to the common human eye, yet comprehensible to him who like Heraclitus resembles the contemplative god. Before his fiery eye no drop of injustice is left in the world poured out around him, and even that cardinal obstacle—how pure fire can take up its quarters in forms so impure—he masters by means of a sublime simile. A Becoming and Passing, a building and destroying, without any moral bias, in perpetual innocence is in this world only the play of the artist and of the child. And similarly, just as the child and the artist play, the eternally living fire plays, builds up and destroys, in innocence—and this game the Æon plays with himself. Transforming himself into water and earth, like a child he piles heaps of sand by the sea, piles up and demolishes; from time to time he recommences the game. A moment of satiety, then again desire seizes him, as desire compels the artist to create. Not wantonness, but the ever newly awakening impulse to play, calls into life other worlds. The child throws away his toys; but soon he starts again in an innocent frame of mind. As soon however as the child builds he connects, joins and forms lawfully and according to an innate sense of order.

Thus, only is the world contemplated by the aesthetic man, who has learned from the artist and the genesis of the latter's work, how the struggle of plurality can yet bear within itself law and justice, how the artist stands contemplative above, and working within the work of art, how necessity and play, antagonism and harmony must pair themselves for the procreation of the work of art.

Who now will still demand from such a philosophy a system of Ethics with the necessary imperatives—Thou Shalt,—or even reproach Heraclitus with such a deficiency. Man down to his last fiber is Necessity and absolutely "unfree "—if by freedom one understands the foolish claim to be able to change at will one's essentia like a garment, a claim, which up to the present every serious philosophy has rejected with due scorn. That so few human beings live with consciousness in the Logos and in accordance with the all-overlooking artist's eye originates from their souls being wet and from the fact that men's eyes and ears, their intellect in general is a bad witness when "moist ooze fills their souls." Why that is so, is not questioned any more than why fire becomes water and earth. Heraclitus is not compelled to prove (as Leibnitz was) that this world was even the best of all; it was sufficient for him that the world is the beautiful, innocent play of the Æon. Man on the whole is to him even an irrational being, with which the fact that in all his essence the law of all-ruling reason is fulfilled does lot clash. He does not occupy a specially favored position in nature, whose highest phenomenon is not simple-minded man, but fire, for instance, as stars. In so far as man has through necessity received a share of fire, he is a little more rational; as far as he consists of earth and water it stands badly with his reason. He is not compelled to take cognizance of the Logos simply because he is a human being. Why is there water, why earth? This to Heraclitus is a much more serious problem than to ask, why men are so stupid and bad. In the highest and the most perverted men the same inherent lawfulness and justice manifest themselves. If, however one would ask Heraclitus the question "Why is fire not always fire, why is it now water, now earth?" then he would only just answer: "It is a game, don't take it too pathetically and still less, morally." Heraclitus describes only the existing world and has the same contemplative pleasure in it which the artist experiences when looking at his growing work. Only those who have cause to be discontented with his natural history of man find him gloomy, melancholy, tearful, somber, atrabilarious, pessimistic and altogether hateful. He however would take these discontented people, together with their antipathies and sympathies, their hatred und their love, as negligible and perhaps answer them with some such comment as: "Dogs bark at anything they do not know," or "To the ass chaff is preferable to gold."

With such discontented persons also originate the numerous complaints as to the obscurity of the Heraclitean style; probably no man has ever written clearer and more illuminatingly; of course, very abruptly, and therefore naturally obscure to the racing readers. But why a philosopher should intentionally write obscurely—a thing habitually said about Heraclitus—is absolutely inexplicable; unless he has some cause to hide his thoughts or is sufficiently a rogue to conceal his thought-lessness underneath words. One is, as Schopenhauer says, indeed compelled by lucid expression to prevent mis-understandings even in affairs of practical every-day life, how then should one be allowed to express oneself indis-tinctly, indeed puzzlingly in the most difficult, most abstruse, scarcely attainable object of thinking, the tasks of philosophy? With respect to brevity however Jean Paul gives a good precept: "On the whole it is right that every-thing great—of deep meaning to a rare mind—should be uttered with brevity and (therefore) obscurely so that the paltry mind would rather proclaim it to be nonsense than translate it into the realm of his empty-headedness. For common minds have an ugly ability to perceive in the deepest and richest saying nothing but their own every-day opinion." Moreover and in spite of it Heraclitus has not escaped the "paltry minds"; already the Stoics have "re-expounded" him into the shallow and dragged down his aesthetic fundamental-perception as to the play of the world to the miserable level of the common regard for the practical ends of the world and more explicitly for the ad-vantages of man, so that out of his Physics has arisen in those heads a crude optimism, with the continual invita-tion to Dick, Tom, and Harry, "Plaudite amici!"

8

Heraclitus was proud; and if it comes to pride with a philosopher then it is a great pride. His work never refers him to a "public," the applause of the masses and the hail-ing chorus of contemporaries. To wander lonely along his path belongs to the nature of the philosopher. His talents are the rarest, in a certain sense the most unnatural and at the same time exclusive and hostile even toward kin-dred talents. The wall of his self-sufficiency must be of diamond, if it is not to be demolished and broken, for everything is in motion against him. His journey to immortality is more cumbersome and impeded than any other and yet nobody can believe more firmly than the philosopher that he will attain the goal by that journey—because he does not know where he is to stand if not on the widely spread wings of all time; for the disregard of everything present and momentary lies in the essence of the great philosophic nature. He has truth; the wheel of time may roll whither it pleases; never can it escape from truth. It is important to hear that such men have lived. Never for example would one be able to imagine the pride of Heraclitus as an idle possibility. In itself every endeavor after knowledge seems by its nature to be eternally unsatisfied and unsatisfactory. Therefore, nobody unless instructed by history will like to believe in such a royal self-esteem and conviction of being the only wooer of truth. Such men live in their own solar-system—one has to look for them there. A Pythagoras, an Empedocles treated themselves too with a super-human esteem, yea, with almost religious awe; but the tie of sympathy united with the great conviction of the metempsychosis and the unity of everything living, led them back to other men, for their welfare and salvation. Of that feeling of solitude, however, which permeated the Ephesian recluse of the Artemis Temple, one can only divine something, when growing benumbed in the wildest mountain desert. No paramount feeling of compassionate agitation, no desire to help, heal and save emanates from him. He is a star without an atmosphere. His eye, directed blazingly inwards, looks outward, for appearance's sake only, extinct and icy. All around him, immediately upon the citadel of his pride beat the waves of folly and perversity: with loathing he turns away from them. But men with a feeling heart would also shun such a Gorgon monster as cast out of brass; within an out-of-the-way sanctuary, among the statues of gods, by the side of cold composedly-sublime architecture such a being may appear more comprehensible. As man among men Heraclitus was incredible; and though he was seen paying attention to the play of noisy children, even then he was reflecting upon what never man thought of on such an occasion: the play of the great world-child, Zeus. He had no need of men, not even for his discernments. He was not interested in all that which one might perhaps ascertain from them, and in what the other sages before him had been endeavoring to ascertain. He spoke with disdain of such questioning, collecting, in short "historic" men. "I sought and investigated myself," he said, with a word by which one designates the investigation of an oracle; as if he and no one else were the true fulfiller and achiever of the Delphic precept: "Know thyself."

What he learned from this oracle, he deemed immortal wisdom, and eternally worthy of explanation, of unlimited effect even in the distance, after the model of the prophetic speeches of the Sibyl. It is sufficient for the latest mankind: let the latter have that expounded to her, as oracular sayings, which he like the Delphic god "neither enunciates nor conceals." Although it is proclaimed by him, "without smiles, finery and the scent of ointments," but rather as with "foaming mouth," it must force its way through the millenniums of the future. For the world needs truth eternally, therefore she needs also Heraclitus eternally; although he has no need of her. What does his fame matter to him?—fame with "mortals ever flowing on!" as he exclaims scornfully. His fame is of concern to man, not to himself; the immortality of mankind needs him, not he the immortality of the man Heraclitus. That which he beheld, the doctrine of the Law in the Becoming, and of the Play in the Necessity, must henceforth be beheld eternally; he has raised the curtain of this greatest stage-play.

9

Whereas in every word of Heraclitus are expressed the pride and the majesty of truth, but of truth caught by intuitions, not scaled by the rope-ladder of Logic, whereas in sublime ecstasy he beholds but does not espy, discerns but does not reckon, he is contrasted with his contemporary Parmenides, a man likewise with the type of a prophet of truth, but formed as it were out of ice and not out of fire, and shedding around himself cold, piercing light.

Parmenides once had, probably in his later years, a moment of the very purest abstraction, undimmed by any reality, perfectly lifeless; this moment—un-Greek, like no other in the two centuries of the Tragic Age—the product of which is the doctrine of "Being," became a boundary-stone for his own life, which divided it into two periods; at the same time however the same moment divides the pre-Socratic thinking into two halves, of which the first might be called the Anaximandrian, the second the Parmenidean. The first period in Parmenides' own philosophizing bears still the signature of Anaximander; this period produced a detailed philosophic-physical system as answer to Anaximander's questions. When later that icy abstraction-horror caught him, and the simplest proposition treating of "Being" and "Not-Being" was advanced by him, then among the many older doctrines thrown by him upon the scrap heap was also his own system. However, he does not appear to have lost all paternal piety towards the strong and well-shaped child of his youth, and he saved himself therefore by saying: "It is true there is only one right way; if one however wants at any time to betake oneself to another, then my earlier opinion according to its purity and consequence alone is right." Sheltering himself with this phrase he has allowed his former physical system a worthy and extensive space in his great poem on Nature, which really was to proclaim the new discernment as the only signpost to truth. This fatherly regard, even though an error should have crept in through it, is a remainder of human feeling, in a nature quite petrified by logical rigidity and almost changed into a thinking-machine.

Parmenides, whose personal intercourse with Anaximander does not seem incredible to me, and whose starting from Anaximander's doctrine is not only credible but evident, had the same distrust for the complete separation of a world which only is, and a world which only becomes, as had also caught Heraclitus and led to a denying of "Being" altogether. Both sought a way out from that contrast and divergence of a dual order of the world. That leap into the Indefinite, Indefinable, by which once for all Anaximander had escaped from the realm of Becoming and from the empirically given qualities of such realm, that leap did not become an easy matter to minds so independently fashioned as those of Heraclitus and Parmenides; first they endeavored to walk as far as they could and reserved to themselves the leap for that place, where the foot finds no more hold and one has to leap, in order not to fall. Both looked repeatedly at that very world, which Anaximander had condemned in so melancholy a way and declared to be the place of wanton crime and at the same time the penitentiary cell for the injustice of Becoming. Contemplating this world Heraclitus, as we know already, had discovered what a wonderful order, regularity and security manifest themselves in every Becoming; from that he concluded that the Becoming could not be anything evil and unjust. Quite a different outlook had Parmenides; he compared the qualities one with another, and believed that they were not all of the same kind, but ought to be classified under two headings. If for example he compared bright and dark, then the second quality was obviously only the negation of the first; and thus, he distinguished positive and negative qualities, seriously endeavoring to rediscover and register that fundamental antithesis in the whole realm of Nature. His method was the following: He took a few antitheses, e.g., light and heavy, rare and dense, active and passive, and compared them with that typical antithesis of bright and dark: that which corresponded with the bright was the positive, that which corresponded with the dark the negative quality. If he took perhaps the heavy and light, the light fell to the side of the bright, the heavy to the side of the dark; and thus "heavy" was to him only the negation of "light," but the "light" a positive quality. This method alone shows that he had a defiant aptitude for abstract logical procedure, closed against the suggestions of the senses. The "heavy" seems indeed to offer itself very forcibly to the senses as a positive quality; that did not keep Parmenides from stamping it as a negation. Similarly he placed the earth in opposition to the fire, the "cold" in opposition to the "warm," the "dense" in opposition to the "rare," the "female" in opposition to the "male," the "passive" in opposition to the "active," merely as negations: so that before his gaze our empiric world divided itself into two separate spheres, into that of the positive qualities—with a bright, fiery, warm, light, rare, active-masculine character—and into that of the negative qualities. The latter express really only the lack, the absence of the others, the positive ones. He therefore described the sphere in which the positive qualities are absent as dark, earthy, cold, heavy, dense and altogether as of feminine-passive character. Instead of the expressions "positive" and "negative" he used the standing term "existent" and "non-existent" and had arrived with this at the proposition, that, in contradiction to Anaximander, this our world itself contains something "existent," and of course something "non-existent." One is not to seek that "existent" outside the world and as it were above our horizon; but before us, and everywhere in every Becoming, something "existent" and active is contained.

With that however still remained to him the task of giving the more exact answer to the question: What is the Becoming? and here was the moment where he had to leap, in order not to fall, although perhaps to such natures as that of Parmenides, even any leaping means a falling. Enough! we get into fog, into the mysticism of qualitates occultæ, and even a little into mythology. Parmenides, like Heraclitus, looks at the general Becoming and Not-remaining and explains to himself a Passing only thus, that the "Non-Existent" bore the guilt. For how should the "Existent" bear the guilt of Passing? Likewise, however, the Originating, i.e., the Becoming, must come about through the assistance of the "Non-Existent"; for the "Existent" is always there and could not of itself first originate and it could not explain any Originating, any Becoming. Therefore, the Originating, the Becoming as well as the Passing and Perishing have been brought about by the negative qualities. But that the originating "thing" has a content, and the passing "thing" loses a content, presupposes that the positive qualities—and that just means that very content—participate likewise in both processes. In short the proposition results: "For the Becoming the 'Existent' as well as the 'Non-Existent' is necessary; when they co-operate then a Becoming results." But how come the "positive" and the "negative" to one another? Should they not on the contrary eternally flee one another as antitheses and thereby make every Becoming impossible? Here Parmenides appeals to a qualitas occulta, to a mystic tendency of the antithetical pairs to approach and attract one another, and he allegorizes that peculiar contrariety by the name of Aphrodite, and by the empirically known relation of the male and female principle. It is the power of Aphrodite which plays the matchmaker between the antithetical pair, the "Existent" and the "Non-Existent." Passion brings together the antagonistic and antipathetic elements: the result is a Becoming. When Desire has become satiated, Hatred and the innate antagonism again drive asunder the "Existent" and the "Non-Existent"—then man says: the thing perishes, passes.

10

But no one with impunity lays his profane hands on such awful abstractions as the "Existent" and the "Non-Existent"; the blood freezes slowly as one touches them. There was a day upon which an odd idea suddenly occurred to Parmenides, an idea which seemed to take all value away from his former combinations, so that he felt inclined to throw them aside, like a money bag with old worn-out coins. It is commonly believed that an external impression, in addition to the centrifugal consequence of such ideas as "existent" and "non-existent," has also been co-active in the invention of that day; this impression was an acquaintance with the theology of the old roamer and rhapsodist, the singer of a mystic deification of Nature, the Kolophonian Xenophanes. Throughout an extraordinary life Xenophanes lived as a wandering poet and became through his travels a well-informed and most instructive man who knew how to question and how to narrate, for which reason Heraclitus reckoned him amongst the polyhistorians and above all amongst the "historic" natures, in the sense mentioned. Whence and when came to him the mystic bent into the One and the eternally Resting, nobody will be able to compute; perhaps it is only the conception of the finally settled old man, to whom, after the agitation of his erratic wanderings, and after the restless learning and searching for truth, the vision of a divine rest, the permanence of all things within a pantheistic primal peace appears as the highest and greatest ideal. After all it seems to me quite accidental that in the same place in Elea two men lived together for a time, each of whom carried in his head a conception of unity; they formed no school and had nothing in common which perhaps the one might have learned from the other and then might have handed on. For, in the case of these two men, the origin of that conception of unity is quite different, yea opposite; and if either of them has become at all acquainted with the doctrine of the other then, in order to understand it at all, he had to translate it first into his own language. With this translation however the very specific element of the other doctrine was lost. Whereas Parmenides arrived at the unity of the "Existent" purely through an alleged logical consequence and whereas he span that unity out of the ideas "Being" and "Not-Being," Xenophanes was a religious mystic and belonged, with that mystic unity, very properly to the Sixth Century. Although he was no such revolutionizing personality as Pythagoras he had nevertheless in his wanderings the same bent and impulse to improve, purify, and cure men. He was the ethical teacher, but still in the stage of the rhapsodist; in a later time, he would have been a sophist. In the daring disapproval of the existing customs and valuations he had not his equal in Greece; moreover he did not, like Heraclitus and Plato, retire into solitude but placed himself before the very public, whose exulting admiration of Homer, whose passionate propensity for the honors of the gymnastic festivals, whose adoration of stones in human shape, he criticized severely with wrath and scorn, yet not as a brawling Thersites. The freedom of the individual was with him on its zenith; and by this almost limitless stepping free from all conventions, he was more closely related to Parmenides than by that last divine unity, which once he had beheld, in a visionary state worthy of that century. His unity scarcely had expression and word in common with the one "Being" of Parmenides, and certainly had not the same origin.

It was rather an opposite state of mind in which Parmenides found his doctrine of "Being," On that day and in that state he examined his two co-operating antitheses, the "Existent" and the "Non-Existent," the positive and the negative qualities, of which Desire and Hatred constitute the world and the Becoming. He was suddenly caught up, mistrusting, by the idea of negative quality, of the "Non-Existent." For can something which does not exist be a quality? or to put the question in a broader sense: can anything indeed which does not exist, exist? The only form of knowledge in which we at once put unconditional trust and the disapproval of which amounts to madness, is the tautology A = A. But this very tautological knowledge called inexorably to him: what does not exist, exists not! What is, is! Suddenly he feels upon his life the load of an enormous logical sin; for had he not always without hesitation assumed that there were existing negative qualities, in short a "Non-Existent," that therefore, to express it by a formula, A = Not-A, which indeed could only be advanced by the most out and out perversity of thinking. It is true, as he recollected, the whole great mass of men judges with the same perversity; he himself has only participated in the general crime against logic. But the same moment which charges him with this crime surrounds him with the light of the glory of an invention, he has found, apart from all human illusion, a principle, the key to the world-secret, he now descends into the abyss of things, guided by the firm and fearful hand of the tautological truth as to "Being."

On the way thither he meets Heraclitus—an unfortunate encounter! Just now Heraclitus' play with antinomies was bound to be very hateful to him, who placed the utmost importance upon the severest separation of "Being" and "Not-Being"; propositions like this: "We are and at the same time we are not" —"'Being' and 'Not-Being' is at the same time the same thing and again not the same thing," propositions through which all that he had just elucidated and disentangled became again dim and inextricable, incited him to wrath. "Away with the men," he exclaimed, "who seem to have two heads and yet know nothing! With them truly everything is in flux, even their thinking! They stare at things stupidly, but they must be deaf as well as blind so to mix up the opposites"! The want of judgment on the part of the masses, glorified by playful antinomies and praised as the acme of all knowledge was to him a painful and incomprehensible experience.

Now he dived into the cold bath of his awful abstractions. That which is true must exist in eternal presence, about it cannot be said "it was," "it will be." The "Existent" cannot have become; for out of what should it have become? Out of the "Non-Existent"? But that does not exist and can produce nothing. Out of the "Existent"? This would not produce anything but itself. The same applies to the Passing, it is just as impossible as the Becoming, as any change, any increase, any decrease. On the whole the proposition is valid: Everything about which it can be said: "it has been" or "it will be" does not exist; about the "Existent" however it can never be said "it does not exist." The "Existent" is indivisible, for where is the second power, which should divide it? It is immovable, for whither should it move itself? It cannot be infinitely great nor infinitely small, for it is perfect and a perfectly given infinitude is a contradiction. Thus the "Existent" is suspended, delimited, perfect, immovable, everywhere equally balanced and such equilibrium equally perfect at any point, like a globe, but not in a space, for otherwise this space would be a second "Existent." But there cannot exist several "Existents," for in order to separate them, something would have to exist which was not existing, an assumption which neutralizes itself. Thus, there exists only the eternal Unity.

If now, however, Parmenides turned back his gaze to the world of Becoming, the existence of which he had formerly tried to understand by such ingenious conjectures, he was wroth at his eye seeing the Becoming at all, his ear hearing it. "Do not follow the dim-sighted eyes," now his command runs, "not the resounding ear nor the tongue, but examine only by the power of the thought." Therewith he accomplished the extremely important first critique of the apparatus of knowledge, although this critique was still inadequate and proved disastrous in its consequences. By tearing entirely asunder the senses and the ability to think in abstractions, i.e., reason, just as if they were two thoroughly separate capacities, he demolished the intellect itself, and incited people to that wholly erroneous separation of "mind" and "body" which, especially since Plato, lies like a curse on philosophy. All sense perceptions, Parmenides judges, cause only illusions and their chief illusion is their deluding us to believe that even the "Non-Existent" exists, that even the Becoming has a "Being." All that plurality, diversity and variety of the empirically known world, the change of its qualities, the order in its ups and downs, is thrown aside mercilessly as mere appearance and delusion; from there nothing is to be learnt, therefore all labour is wasted which one bestows upon this false, through-and-through futile world, the conception of which has been obtained by being humbugged by the senses. He who judges in such generalizations as Parmenides did, ceases therewith to be an investigator of natural philosophy in detail; his interest in phenomena withers away; there develops even a hatred of being unable to get rid of this eternal fraud of the senses. Truth is now to dwell only in the most faded, most abstract generalities, in the empty husks of the most indefinite words, as in a maze of cobwebs; and by such a "truth" now the philosopher sits, bloodless as an abstraction and surrounded by a web of formulae. The spider undoubtedly wants the blood of its victims; but the Parmenidean philosopher hates the very blood of his victims, the blood of Empiricism sacrificed by him.

Zeno of Elea by Jan de Bisschop

11

And that was a Greek who "flourished" about the time of the outbreak of the Ionic Revolution. At that time it was possible for a Greek to flee out of the superabundant reality, as out of a mere delusive schematism of the imaginative faculties—not perhaps like Plato into the land of the eternal ideas, into the workshop of the world-creator, in order to feast the eyes on unblemished, unbreakable primal-forms of things—but into the rigid death-like rest of the coldest and emptiest conception, that of the "Being." We will indeed beware of interpreting such a remarkable fact by false analogies. That flight was not a world-flight in the sense of Indian philosophers; no deep religious conviction as to the depravity, transitoriness and accursedness of Existence demanded that flight—that ultimate goal, the rest in the "Being," was not striven after as the mystic absorption in one all-sufficing enrapturing conception which is a puzzle and a scandal to common men. The thought of Parmenides bears in itself not the slightest trace of the intoxicating mystical Indian fragrance, which is perhaps not wholly imperceptible in Pythagoras and Empedocles; the strange thing in that fact, at this period, is rather the very absence of fragrance, color, soul, form, the total lack of blood, religiosity and ethical warmth, the abstract-schematic—in a Greek!—above all however our philosopher's awful energy of striving after Certainty, in a mythically thinking and highly emotional—fantastic age is quite remarkable. "Grant me but a certainty, ye gods!" is the prayer of Parmenides, "and be it, in the ocean of Uncertainty, only a board, broad enough to lie on! Everything becoming, everything luxuriant, varied, blossoming, deceiving, stimulating, living, take all that for yourselves, and give to me but the single poor empty Certainty!"

In the philosophy of Parmenides, the theme of ontology forms the prelude. Experience offered him nowhere a

"Being" as he imagined it to himself, but from the fact that he could conceive of it he concluded that it must exist; a conclusion which rests upon the supposition that we have an organ of knowledge which reaches into the nature of things and is independent of experience. The material of our thinking according to Parmenides does not exist in perception at all but is brought in from somewhere else, from an extra-material world to which by thinking we have a direct access. Against all similar chains of reasoning Aristotle has already asserted that existence never belongs to the essence, never belongs to the nature of a thing. For that very reason from the idea of "Being"—of which the essentia precisely is only the "Being"—cannot be inferred an existentia of the "Being" at all. The logical content of that antithesis "Being" and "Not-Being" is perfectly nil, if the object lying at the bottom of it, if the precept cannot be given from which this antithesis has been deduced by abstraction; without this going back to the precept the antithesis is only a play with conceptions, through which indeed nothing is discerned. For the merely logical criterion of truth, as Kant teaches, namely the agreement of a discernment with the general and the formal laws of intellect and reason is, it is true, the conditio sine qua non, consequently the negative condition of all truth; further however logic cannot go, and logic cannot discover by any touchstone the error which pertains not to the form but to the contents. As soon, however, as one seeks the content for the logical truth of the antithesis: "That which is, is; that which is not, is not," one will find indeed not a simple reality, which is fashioned rigidly according to that antithesis: about a tree I can say as well "it is" in comparison with all the other things, as well "it becomes" in comparison with itself at another moment of time as finally also "it is not," e.g.," it is not yet tree," as long as I perhaps look at the shrub. Words are only symbols for the relations of things among themselves and to us, and nowhere touch absolute truth; and now to crown all, the word "Being" designates only the most general relation, which connects all things, and so does the word "Not-Being." If, however the Existence of the things themselves be unprovable, then the relation of the things among themselves, the so-called "Being" and "Not-Being," will not bring us any nearer to the land of truth. By means of words and ideas we shall never get behind the wall of the relations, let us say into some fabulous primal cause of things, and even in the pure forms of the sensitive faculty and of the intellect, in space, time and causality we gain nothing, which might resemble a "Veritas æterna?" It is absolutely impossible for the subject to see and discern something beyond himself, so impossible that Cognition and "Being" are the most contradictory of all spheres. And if in the uninstructed naïveté of the then critique of the intellect Parmenides was permitted to fancy that out of the eternally subjective idea he had come to a "Being-In-itself," then it is to-day, after Kant, a daring ignorance, if here and there, especially among badly informed theologians who want to play the philosopher, is proposed as the task of philosophy: "to conceive the Absolute by means of consciousness," perhaps even in the form: "the Absolute is already extant, else how could it be sought?" as Hegel has expressed himself, or with the saying of Beneke: "that the 'Being' must be given somehow, must be attainable for us somehow, since otherwise we could not even have the idea of 'Being.'" The idea of "Being"! As though that idea did not indicate the most miserable empiric origin already in the etymology of the word. For esse means at the bottom: "to breathe," if man uses it of all other things, then he transmits the conviction that he himself breathes and lives by means of a metaphor, i.e., by means of something illogical to the other things and conceives of their Existence as a Breathing according to human analogy. Now the original meaning of the word soon becomes effaced; so much however still remains that man conceives of the existence of other things according to the analogy of his own existence, therefore anthropomorphically, and at any rate by means of an illogical transmission. Even to man, therefore apart from that transmission, the proposition: "I breathe, therefore a 'Being' exists" is quite insufficient since against it the same objection must be made, as against the ambulo, ergo sum, or ergo est.

12

The other idea, of greater import than that of the "Existent," and likewise invented already by Parmenides, although not yet so clearly applied as by his disciple Zeno is the idea of the Infinite. Nothing Infinite can exist; for from such an assumption the contradictory idea of a perfect Infinitude would result. Since now our actuality, our existing world everywhere shows the character of that perfect Infinitude, our world signifies in its nature a contradiction against logic and therewith also against reality and is deception, lie, fantasma. Zeno especially applied the method of indirect proof; he said for example, "There can be no motion from one place to another; for if there were such a motion, then an Infinitude would be given as perfect, this however is an impossibility." Achilles cannot catch up the tortoise which has a small start in a race, for in order to reach only the point from which the tortoise began, he would have had to run through innumerable, infinitely many spaces, viz., first half of that space, then the fourth, then the sixteenth, and so on ad infinitum. If he does in fact overtake the tortoise then this is an illogical phenomenon, and therefore at any rate not a truth, not a reality, not real "Being," but only a delusion. For it is never possible to finish the infinite. Another popular expression of this doctrine is the flying and yet resting arrow. At any instant of its flight, it has a position; in this position it rests. Now would the sum of the infinite positions of rest be identical with motion? Would now the

Resting, infinitely often repeated, be Motion, therefore its own opposite? The Infinite is here used as the aqua fortis of reality, through it the latter is dissolved. If however the Ideas are fixed, eternal and entitative—and for Parmenides "Being" and Thinking coincide—if therefore the Infinite can never be perfect, if Rest can never become Motion, then in fact the arrow has not flown at all; it never left its place and resting position; no moment of time has passed. Or expressed in another way: in this so-called yet only alleged Actuality there exists neither time, nor space, nor motion. Finally, the arrow itself is only an illusion; for it originates out of the Plurality, out of the phantasmagoria of the "Non-One" produced by the senses. Suppose the arrow had a "Being," then it would be immovable, timeless, increate, rigid and eternal—an impossible conception! Supposing that Motion was truly real, then there would be no rest, therefore no position for the arrow, therefore no space— an impossible conception! Supposing that time were real, then it could not be of an infinite divisibility; the time which the arrow needed, would have to consist of a limited number of time-moments, each of these moments would have to be an Atomon—an impossible conception! All our conceptions, as soon as their empirically-given content, drawn out of this concrete world, is taken as a Veritas æterna, lead to contradictions. If there is absolute motion, then there is no space; if there is absolute space then there is no motion; if there is absolute "Being," then there is no Plurality; if there is an absolute Plurality, then there is no Unity. It should at least become clear to us how little we touch the heart of things or untie the knot of reality with such ideas, whereas Parmenides and Zeno inversely hold fast to the truth and omnivalidity of ideas and condemn the perceptible world as the opposite of the true and om-nivalid ideas, as an objectivation of the illogical and contradictory. With all their proofs they start from the wholly indemonstrable, yea improbable assumption that in that apprehensive faculty we possess the decisive, highest criterion of "Being" and "Not-Being," i.e., of objective reality and its opposite; those ideas are not to prove themselves true, to correct themselves by Actuality, as they are after all really derived from it, but on the contrary they are to measure and to judge Actuality, and in case of a contradiction with logic, even to condemn. In order to concede to them this judicial competence Parmenides had to ascribe to them the same "Being," which alone he allowed in general as the "Being"; Thinking and that one increate perfect ball of the "Existent" were now no longer to be conceived as two different kinds of "Being," since there was not permitted a duality of "Being." Thus the over-risky flash of fancy had become necessary to declare Thinking and "Being" identical. No form of perceptibility, no symbol, no simile could possibly be of any help here; the fancy was wholly inconceivable, but it was necessary, yea in the lack of every possibility of illustration it celebrated the highest triumph over the world and the claims of the senses. Thinking and that clod-like, ball-shaped, through-and-through dead-massive, and rigid-immovable "Being," must, according to the Parmenidean imperative, dissolve into one another and be the same in every respect, to the horror of fantasy. What does it matter that this identity contradicts the senses! This contradiction is just the guarantee that such an identity is not borrowed from the senses.

13

Moreover against Parmenides could be produced a strong couple of argumenta ad hominem or ex concessis, by which, it is true, truth itself could not be brought to light, but at any rate the untruth of that absolute separation of the world of the senses and the world of the ideas, and the untruth of the identity of "Being" and Thinking could be demonstrated. Firstly, if the Thinking of Reason in ideas is real, then also Plurality and Motion must have reality, for rational Thinking is mobile; and more precisely, it is a motion from idea to idea, therefore within a plurality of realities. There is no subterfuge against that; it is quite impossible to designate Thinking as a rigid Permanence, as an eternally immobile, intellectual Introspection of Unity. Secondly, if only fraud and illusion come from the senses, and if in reality there exists only the real identity of "Being" and Thinking, what then are the senses themselves? They too are certainly Appearance only since they do not coincide with the Thinking, and their product, the world of senses, does not coincide with "Being." If however the senses themselves are Appearance to whom then are they Appearance? How can they, being unreal, still deceive? The "Non-Existent" cannot even deceive. Therefore the Whence? of deception and Appearance remains an enigma, yea, a contradiction. We call these argumenta ad hominem: The Objection Of The Mobile Reason and that of The Origin Of Appearance. From the first would result the reality of Motion and of Plurality, from the second the impossibility of the Parmenidean Appearance, assuming that the chief-doctrine of Parmenides on the "Being" were accepted as true. This chief-doctrine however only says: The "Existent" only has a "Being," the "Non-Existent" does not exist. If Motion however has such a "Being," then to Motion applies what applies to the "Existent" in general: it is increate, eternal, indestructible, without increase or decrease. But if the "Appearance" is denied and a belief in it made untenable, by means of that question as to the Whence? of the "Appearance," if the stage of the so-called Becoming, of change, our many-shaped, restless, colored and rich Existence is protected from the Parmenidean rejection, then it is necessary to characterize this world of change and alteration as a sum of such really existing Essentials, existing simultaneously into all eternity. Of a change in the strict sense, of a Becoming there cannot naturally be any question even with this assumption. But now

Plurality has a real "Being," all qualities have a real "Being" and motion not less; and of any moment of this world— although these moments chosen at random lie at a distance of millenniums from one another—it would have to be possible to say: all real Essentials extant in this world are without exception co-existent, unaltered, undiminished, without increase, without decrease. A millennium later the world is exactly the same. Nothing has altered. If in spite of that the appearance of the world at the one time is quite different from that at the other time, then that is no deception, nothing merely apparent, but the effect of eternal motion. The real "Existent" is moved sometimes thus, sometimes thus: together, asunder, upwards, downwards, into one another, pell-mell.

14

With this conception we have already taken a step into the realm of the doctrine of Anaxagoras. By him both objections against Parmenides are raised in full strength; that of the mobile Thinking and that of the Whence? of "Appearance"; but in the chief proposition Parmenides has subjugated him as well as all the younger philosophers and nature-explorers. They all deny the possibility of Becoming and Passing, as the mind of the people conceives them and as Anaximander and Heraclitus had assumed with greater circumspection and yet still heedlessly. Such a mythological Originating out of the Nothing, such a Disappearing into the Nothing, such an arbitrary Changing of the Nothing into the Something, such a random exchanging, putting on and putting off of the qualities was henceforth considered senseless; but so was, and for the same reasons, an originating of the Many out of the One, of the manifold qualities out of the one primal-quality, in short the derivation of the world out of a primary substance, as argued by Thales and Heraclitus. Rather was now the real problem advanced of applying the doctrine of increate imperishable "Being" to this existing world, without taking one's refuge in the theory of appearance and deception. But if the empiric world is not to be Appearance, if the things are not to be derived out of Nothing and just as little out of the one Something, then these things must contain in themselves a real "Being," their matter and content must be unconditionally real, and all change can refer only to the form, i.e., to the position, order, grouping, mixing, separation of these eternally co-existing Essentials. It is just as in a game of dice; they are ever the same dice; but falling sometimes thus, sometimes thus, they mean to us something different. All older theories had gone back to a primal element, as womb and cause of Becoming, be this water, air, fire or the Indefinite of Anaximander. Against that Anaxagoras now asserts that out of the Equal the Unequal could never come forth, and that out of the one "Existent" the change could never be explained. Whether now one were to imagine that assumed matter to be rarefied or condensed, one would never succeed by such a condensation or rarefaction in explaining the problem one would like to explain: the plurality of qualities.

But if the world in fact is full of the most different qualities then these must, in case they are not appearance, have a "Being," i.e., must be eternal, increate, imperishable and ever co-existing. Appearance, however, they cannot be, since the question as to the Whence? of Appearance remains unanswered, yea answers itself in the negative! The earlier seekers after Truth had intended to simplify the problem of Becoming by advancing only one substance, which bore in its bosom the possibilities of all Becoming; now on the contrary it is asserted: there are innumerable substances, but never more, never less, and never new ones. Only Motion, playing dice with them throws them into ever new combinations. That Motion however is a truth and not Appearance, Anaxagoras proved in opposition to Parmenides by the indisputable succession of our conceptions in thinking. We have therefore in the most direct fashion the insight into the truth of motion and succession in the fact that we think and have conceptions. Therefore at any rate the one rigid, resting, dead "Being" of Parmenides has been removed out of the way, there are many "Existents" just as surely as all these many "Existents" (existing things, substances) are in motion. Change is motion—but whence originates motion? Does this motion leave perhaps wholly untouched the proper essence of those many independent, isolated substances, and, according to the most severe idea of the "Existent," must not motion in itself be foreign to them? Or does it after all belong to the things themselves? We stand here at an important decision; according to which way we turn, we shall step into the realm either of Anaxagoras or of Empedocles or of Democritus. The delicate question must be raised: if there are many substances, and if these many move, what moves them? Do they move one another? Or is it perhaps only gravitation? Or are there magic forces of attraction and repulsion within the things themselves? Or does the cause of motion lie outside these many real substances? Or putting the question more pointedly: if two things show a succession, a mutual change of position, does that originate from themselves? And is this to be explained mechanically or magically?

Or if this should not be the case is it a third something which moves them? It is a sorry problem, for Parmenides would still have been able to prove against Anaxagoras the impossibility of motion, even granted that there are many substances. For he could say: Take two Substances existing of themselves, each with quite differently fashioned, autonomous, unconditioned "Being"—and of such kind are the Anaxagorean substances—they can never clash together, never move, never attract one another, there exists between them no causality, no bridge, they do not come into contact with one another, do not disturb one another, they do not interest one another, they are utterly indifferent. The impact then is just as inexplicable as the magic attraction: that which is utterly foreign cannot exercise any effect upon another, therefore cannot move itself nor allow itself to be moved. Parmenides would even have added: the only way of escape which is left to you is this, to ascribe motion to the things themselves; then however all that you know and see as motion is indeed only a deception and not true motion, for the only kind of motion which could belong to those absolutely original substances, would be merely an autogenous motion limited to themselves without any effect. But you assume motion in order to explain those effects of change, of the disarrangement in space, of alteration, in short the causalities and relations of the things among themselves. But these very effects would not be explained and would remain as problematic as ever; for this reason one cannot conceive why it should be necessary to assume a motion since it does not perform that which you demand from it. Motion does not belong to the nature of things and is eternally foreign to them.

Those opponents of the Eleatean unmoved Unity were induced to make light of such an argument by prejudices of a perceptual character. It seems so irrefutable that each veritable "Existent" is a space-filling body, a lump of matter, large or small but in any case spatially dimensioned; so that two or more such lumps cannot be in one space. Under this hypothesis Anaxagoras, as later on Democritus, assumed that they must knock against each other; if in their motions they came by chance upon one another, that they would dispute the same space with each other, and that this struggle was the very cause of all Change. In other words: those wholly isolated, thoroughly heterogeneous and eternally unalterable substances were after all not conceived as being absolutely heterogeneous but all had in addition to a specific, wholly peculiar quality, also one absolutely homogeneous substratum: a piece of

114

space-filling matter. In their participation in matter they all stood equal and therefore could act upon one another, i.e., knock one another. Moreover all Change did not in the least depend on the heterogeneity of those substances but on their homogeneity, as matter. At the bottom of the assumption of Anaxagoras is a logical oversight; for that which is the "Existent-In-Itself" must be wholly unconditional and coherent, is therefore not allowed to assume as its cause anything,—whereas all those Anaxagorean substances have still a conditioning Something: matter, and already assume its existence; the substance "Red" for example was to Anaxagoras not just merely red in itself but also in a reserved or suppressed way a piece of matter without any qualities. Only with this matter the "Red-In-Itself" acted upon other substances, not with the "Red," but with that which is not red, not colored, nor in any way qualitatively definite. If the "Red" had been taken strictly as "Red," as the real substance itself, therefore without that substratum, then Anaxagoras would certainly not have dared to speak of an effect of the "Red" upon other substances, perhaps even with the phrase that the "Red-In-Itself" was transmitting the impact received from the "Fleshy-In-Itself." Then it would be clear that such an "Existent" par excellence could never be moved.

15

One has to glance at the opponents of the Eleates, in order to appreciate the extraordinary advantages in the assumption of Parmenides. What embarrassments,—from which Parmenides had escaped,—awaited Anaxagoras and all who believed in a plurality of substances, with the question, How many substances? Anaxagoras made the leap, closed his eyes and said, "Infinitely many"; thus he had flown at least beyond the incredibly laborious proof of a definite number of elementary substances. Since these

"Infinitely Many" had to exist without increase and unaltered for eternities, in that assumption was given the contradiction of an infinity to be conceived as completed and perfect. In short, Plurality, Motion, Infinity driven into flight by Parmenides with the amazing proposition of the one "Being," returned from their exile and hurled their projectiles at the opponents of Parmenides, causing them wounds for which there is no cure. Obviously those opponents have no real consciousness and knowledge as to the awful force of those Eleatean thoughts, "There can be no time, no motion, no space; for all these we can only think of as infinite, and to be more explicit, firstly infinitely large, then infinitely divisible; but everything infinite has no 'Being,' does not exist," and this nobody doubts, who takes the meaning of the word "Being" severely and considers the existence of something contradictory impossible, e.g., the existence of a completed infinity. If however the very Actuality shows us everything under the form of the completed infinity then it becomes evident that it contradicts itself and therefore has no true reality. If those opponents however should object: "but in your thinking itself there does exist succession, therefore neither could your thinking be real and consequently could not prove anything," then Parmenides perhaps like Kant in a similar case of an equal objection would have answered: "I can, it is true, say my conceptions follow upon one another, but that means only that we are not conscious of them unless within a chronological order, i.e., according to the form of the inner sense. For that reason time is not a something in itself nor any order or quality objectively adherent to things." We should therefore have to distinguish between the Pure Thinking, that would be timeless like the one Parmenidean "Being," and the consciousness of this thinking, and the latter would already translate the thinking into the form of appearance, i.e., of succession, plurality and motion. It is probable that Parmenides would have availed himself of this loophole; however, the same objection would then have to be raised against him which is raised against Kant by A. Spir ("Thinking And Reality," 2nd ed., vol. i., pp. 209, &c). "Now, in the first place however it is clear, that I cannot know anything of a succession as such, unless I have the successive members of the same simultaneously in my consciousness. Thus the conception of a succession itself is not at all successive, hence also quite different from the succession of our conceptions. Secondly Kant's assumption implies such obvious absurdities that one is surprised that he could leave them unnoticed. Cæsar and Socrates according to this assumption are not really dead, they still live exactly as they did two thousand years ago and only seem to be dead, as a consequence of an organization of my inner sense." Future men already live and if they do not now step forward as living that organization of the "inner sense" is likewise the cause of it. Here above all other things the question is to be put: How can the beginning and the end of conscious life itself, together with all its internal and external senses, exist merely in the conception of the inner sense? The fact is indeed this, that one certainly cannot deny the reality of Change. If it is thrown out through the window it slips in again through the keyhole. If one says: "It merely seems to me, that conditions and conceptions change,"—then this very semblance and appearance itself is something objectively existing and within it without doubt the succession has objective reality, some things in it really do succeed one another.— Besides one must observe that indeed the whole critique of reason only has cause and right of existence under the assumption that to us our conceptions themselves appear exactly as they are. For if the conceptions also appeared to us otherwise than they really are, then one would not be able to advance any solid proposition about them, and therefore would not be able to accomplish any gnosiology or any "transcendental" investigation of objective validity. Now it remains however beyond all doubt that our conceptions themselves appear to us as successive."

The contemplation of this undoubted succession and agitation has now urged Anaxagoras to a memorable hypothesis. Obviously the conceptions themselves moved themselves, were not pushed and had no cause of motion outside themselves. Therefore he said to himself, there exists a something which bears in itself the origin and the commencement of motion; secondly, however, he notices that this conception was moving not only itself but also something quite different, the body. He discovers therefore, in the most immediate experience an effect of conceptions upon expansive matter, which makes itself known as motion in the latter. That was to him a fact; and only incidentally it stimulated him to explain this fact. Let it suffice that he had a regulative schema for the motion in the world,—this motion he now understood either as a motion of the true isolated essences through the Conceptual Principle, the Nous, or as a motion through a something already moved. That with his fundamental assumption the latter kind, the mechanical transmission of motions and impacts likewise contained in itself a problem, probably escaped him; the commonness and everyday occurrence of the effect through impact most probably dulled his eye to the mysteriousness of impact. On the other hand he certainly felt the problematic, even contradictory nature of an effect of conceptions upon substances existing in themselves and he also tried therefore to trace this effect back to a mechanical push and impact which were considered by him as quite comprehensible. For the Nous too was without doubt such a substance existing in itself and was characterized by him as a very delicate and subtle matter, with the specific quality of thinking. With a character assumed in this way, the effect of this matter upon other matter had of course to be of exactly the same kind as that which another substance exercises upon a third, i.e., a mechanical effect, moving by pressure and impact. Still the philosopher had now a substance which moves itself and other things, a substance of which the motion did not come from outside and depended on no one else: whereas it seemed almost a matter of indifference how this automobilism was to be conceived of, perhaps similar to that pushing themselves hither and thither of very fragile and small globules of quicksilver. Among all questions which concern motion there is none more troublesome than the question as to the beginning of motion. For if one may be allowed to conceive of all remaining motions as effect and consequences, then nevertheless the first primal motion is still to be explained; for the mechanical motions, the first link of the chain certainly cannot lie in a mechanical motion, since that would be as good as recurring to the nonsensical idea of the causa sui. But likewise it is not feasible to attribute to the eternal, unconditional things a motion of their own, as it were from the beginning, as dowry of their existence. For motion cannot be conceived without a direction whither and whereupon, therefore only as relation and condition; but a thing is no longer "entitative-in-itself" and "unconditional," if according to its nature it refers necessarily to something existing outside of it. In this embarrassment Anaxagoras thought he had found an extraordinary help and salvation in that Nous, automobile and otherwise independent; the nature of that Nous being just obscure and veiled enough to produce the deception about it, that its assumption also involves that forbidden causa sui. To empiric observation it is even an established fact that Conception is not a causa sui but the effect of the brain, yea, it must appear to that observation as an odd eccentricity to separate the "mind," the product of the brain, from its causa and still to deem it existing after this severing. This Anaxagoras did; he forgot the brain, its marvelous design, the delicacy and intricacy of its convolutions and passages and he decreed the "Mind-In-Itself." This "Mind-In-Itself" alone among all substances had Free-will,—a grand discernment! This Mind was able at any odd time to begin with the motion of the things outside it; on the other hand for ages and ages it could occupy itself with itself—in short Anaxagoras was allowed to assume a first moment of motion in some primeval age, as the Chalaza of all so-called Becoming; i.e., of all Change, namely of all shifting and rearranging of the eternal substances and their particles, Although the Mind itself is eternal, it is in no way compelled to torment itself for eternities with the shifting about of grains of matter; and certainly there was a time and a state of those matters—it is quite indifferent whether that time was of long or short duration—during which the Nous had not acted upon them, during which they were still unmoved. That is the period of the Anaxagorean chaos.

16

The Anaxagorean chaos is not an immediately evident conception; in order to grasp it one must have understood the conception which our philosopher had with respect to the so-called "Becoming." For in itself the state of all heterogeneous "Elementary-existences" before all motion would by no means necessarily result in an absolute mixture of all "seeds of things," as the expression of Anaxagoras runs, an intermixture, which he imagined as a complete pell-mell, disordered in its smallest parts, after all these "Elementary-existences" had been, as in a mortar, pounded and resolved into atoms of dust, so that now in that chaos, as in an amphora, they could be whirled into a medley. One might say that this conception of the chaos did not contain anything inevitable, that one merely needed rather to assume any chance position of all those "existences," but not an infinite decomposition of them; an irregular side-by-side arrangement was already sufficient; there was no need of a pell-mell, let alone such a total pell-mell. What therefore put into Anaxagoras' head that difficult and complex conception? As already said: his conception of the empirically given Becoming. From his experience he drew first a most extraordinary proposition on the Becoming, and this proposition necessarily resulted in that doctrine of the chaos, as its consequence.

The observation of the processes of evolution in nature, not a consideration of an earlier philosophical system, suggested to Anaxagoras the doctrine, that All originated from All; this was the conviction of the natural philosopher based upon a manifold, and at the bottom, of course, excessively inadequate induction. He proved it thus: if even the contrary could originate out of the contrary, e.g., the Black out of the White, everything is possible; that however did happen with the dissolution of white snow into black water. The nourishment of the body he explained to himself in this way: that in the articles of food there must be invisibly small constituents of flesh or blood or bone which during alimentation became disengaged and united with the homogeneous in the body. But if All can become out of All, the Firm out of the Liquid, the Hard out of the Soft, the Black out of the White, the Fleshy out of Bread, then also All must be contained in All. The names of things in that case express only the preponderance of the one substance over the other substances to be met with in smaller, often imperceptible quantities. In gold, that is to say, in that which one designates a potiore by the name "gold," there must be also contained silver, snow, bread, and flesh, but in very small quantities; the whole is called after the preponderating item, the gold-substance.

But how is it possible, that one substance preponderates and fills a thing in greater mass than the others present? Experience shows, that this preponderance is gradually produced only through Motion, that the preponderance is the result of a process, which we commonly call Becoming. On the other hand, that "All is in All" is not the result of a process, but, on the contrary, the preliminary condition of all Becoming and all Motion, and is consequently previous to all Becoming. In other words: experience teaches, that continually the like is added to the like, e.g., through nourishment, therefore originally those homogeneous substances were not together and agglomerated, but they were separate. Rather, in all empiric processes coming before our eyes, the homogeneous is always segregated from the heterogeneous and transmitted (e.g., during nourishment, the particles of flesh out of the bread, &c), consequently the pell-mell of the different substances is the older form of the constitution of things and in point of time previous to all Becoming and Moving. If all so-called Becoming is a segregating and presupposes a mixture, the question arises, what degree of intermixture this pell-mell must have had originally. Although the process of a moving on the part of the homogeneous to the homogeneous—i.e., Becoming—has already lasted an immense time, one recognizes in spite of that, that even yet in all things remainders and seed-grains of all other things are enclosed, waiting for their segregation, and one recognizes further that only here and there a preponderance has been brought about; the primal mixture must have been a complete one, i.e., going down to the infinitely small, since the separation and unmixing takes up an infinite length of time. Thereby strict adherence is paid to the thought: that everything which possesses an essential "Being" is infinitely divisible, without forfeiting its specificum.

According to these hypotheses Anaxagoras conceives of the world's primal existence: perhaps as similar to a dust-like mass of infinitely small, concrete particles of which every one is specifically simple and possesses one quality only, yet so arranged that every specific quality is represented in an infinite number of individual particles. Such particles Aristotle has called Homoiomere in consideration of the fact that they are the Parts, all equal one to another, of a Whole which is homogeneous with its Parts. One would however commit a serious mistake to equate this primal pell-mell of all such particles, such "seed-grains of things" to the one primal matter of Anaximander; for the latter's primal matter called the "Indefinite" is a thoroughly coherent and peculiar mass, the former's primal pell-mell is an aggregate of substances. It is true one can assert about this Aggregate of Substances exactly the same as about the Indefinite of Anaximander, as Aristotle does: it could be neither white nor grey, nor black, nor of any other color; it was tasteless, scentless, and altogether as a Whole defined neither quantitatively nor qualitatively: so far goes the similarity of the Anaximandrian Indefinite and the Anaxagorean Primal Mixture. But disregarding this negative equality they distinguish themselves one from another positively by the latter being a compound, the former a unity. Anaxagoras had by the assumption of his Chaos at least so much to his advantage, that he was not compelled to deduce the Many from the One, the Becoming out of the "Existent."

Of course with his complete intermixture of the "seeds" he had to admit one exception: the Nous was not then, nor is It now admixed with any thing. For if It were admixed with only one "Existent," It would have, in infinite divisions, to dwell in all things. This exception is logically very dubious, especially considering the previously described material nature of the Nous, it has something mythological in itself and seems arbitrary, but was however, according to Anaxagorean prœmissa, a strict necessity. The Mind, which is moreover infinitely divisible like any other matter, only not through other matters but through Itself, has, if It divides Itself, in dividing and conglobating sometimes in large, sometimes in small masses, Its equal mass and quality from all eternity; and that which at this minute exists as Mind in animals, plants, men, was also Mind without a more or less, although distributed in another way a thousand years ago. But wherever It had a relation to another substance, there It never was admixed with it, but voluntarily seized it, moved and pushed it arbitrarily—

in short, ruled it. Mind, which alone has motion in Itself, alone possesses ruling power in this world and shows it through moving the grains of matter. But whither does It move them? Or is a motion conceivable, without direction, without path? Is Mind in Its impacts just as arbitrary as it is, with regard to the time when It pushes, and when It does not push? In short, does Chance, i.e., the blindest option, rule within Motion? At this boundary we step into the Most Holy within the conceptual realm of Anaxagoras.

17

What had to be done with that chaotic pell-mell of the primal state previous to all motion, so that out of it, without any increase of new substances and forces, the existing world might originate, with its regular stellar orbits, with its regulated forms of seasons and days, with its manifold beauty and order,—in short, so that out of the Chaos might come a Cosmos? This can be only the effect of Motion, and of a definite and well-organized motion. This Motion itself is the means of the Nous, Its goal would be the perfect segregation of the homogeneous, a goal up to the present not yet attained, because the disorder and the mixture in the beginning was infinite. This goal is to be striven after only by an enormous process, not to be realized suddenly by a mythological stroke of the wand. If ever, at an infinitely distant point of time, it is achieved that everything homogeneous is brought together and the "primal-existences" undivided are encamped side by side in beautiful order, and every particle has found its comrades and its home, and the great peace comes about after the great division and splitting up of the substances, and there will be no longer anything that is divided and split up, then the Nous will again return into Its automobilism and, no longer Itself divided, roam through the world, sometimes in larger, sometimes in smaller masses, as plant-mind or animal-mind, and no longer will It take up Its new dwelling-place in other matter. Meanwhile the task has not been completed; but the kind of motion which the Nous has thought out, in order to solve the task, shows a marvelous suitableness, for by this motion the task is further solved in each new moment. For this motion has the character of concentrically progressive circular motion; it began at some one point of the chaotic mixture, in the form of a little gyration, and in ever larger paths this circular movement traverses all existing "Being," jerking forth everywhere the homogeneous to the homogeneous. At first this revolution brings everything Dense to the Dense, everything Rare to the Rare, and likewise all that is Dark, Bright, Moist, Dry to their kind; above these general groups or classifications there are again two still more comprehensive, namely Ether, that is to say everything that is Warm, Bright, Rare, and Aër, that is to say everything that is Dark, Cold, Heavy, Firm. Through the segregation of the ethereal masses from the aerial, there is formed, as the most immediate effect of that epicycle whose center moves along in the circumference of ever greater circles, a something as in an eddy made in standing water; heavy compounds are led towards the middle and compressed. Just in the same way that travelling waterspout in chaos forms itself on the outer side out of the Ethereal, Rare, Bright Constituents, on the inner side out of the Cloudy, Heavy, Moist Constituents. Then in the course of this process out of that Aerial mass, conglomerating in its interior, water is separated, and again out of the water the earthy element, and then out of the earthy element, under the effect of the awful cold are separated the stones. Again at some juncture masses of stone, through the momentum of the rotation, are torn away sideways from the earth and thrown into the realm of the hot light Ether; there in the latter's fiery element they are made to glow and, carried along in the ethereal rotation, they irradiate light, and as sun and stars illuminate and warm the earth, in herself dark and cold. The whole conception is of a wonderful daring and simplicity and has nothing of that clumsy and anthropomorphical teleology, which has been frequently connected with the name of Anaxagoras. That conception has its greatness just in this, that it derives the whole Cosmos of Becoming out of the moved circle, whereas Parmenides contemplated the true "Existent" as a resting, dead ball. Once that circle is put into motion and caused to roll by the Nous, then all the order, law and beauty of the world is the natural consequence of that first impetus. How very much one wrongs Anaxagoras if one reproaches him for the wise abstention from teleology which shows itself in this conception and talks scornfully of his Nous as of a deus ex machina. Rather, on account of the elimination of mythological and theistic miracle-working and anthropomorphic ends and utilities, Anaxagoras might have made use of proud words similar to those which Kant used in his Natural History of the Heavens. For it is indeed a sublime thought, to retrace that grandeur of the cosmos and the marvelous arrangement of the orbits of the stars, to retrace all that, in all forms to a simple, purely mechanical motion and, as it were, to a moved mathematical figure, and therefore not to reduce all that to purposes and intervening hands of a machine-god, but only to a kind of oscillation, which, having once begun, is in its progress necessary and definite, and effects result which resemble the wisest computation of sagacity and extremely well thought-out fitness without being anything of the sort. "I enjoy the pleasure," says Kant, of seeing how a well-ordered whole produces itself without the assistance of arbitrary fabrications, under the impulse of fixed laws of motion—a well-ordered whole which looks so similar to that world-system which is ours, that I cannot abstain from considering it to be the same. It seems to me that one might say here, in a certain sense without presumption: 'Give me matter and I will build a world out of it.'"

18

Suppose now, that for once we allow that primal mixture as rightly concluded, some considerations especially
from Mechanics seem to oppose the grand plan of the
world edifice. For even though the Mind at a point causes
a circular movement its continuation is only conceivable
with great difficulty, especially since it is to be infinite and
gradually to make all existing masses rotate. As a matter
of course one would assume that the pressure of all the
remaining matter would have crushed out this small circular movement when it had scarcely begun; that this
does not happen presupposes on the part of the stimulating Nous, that the latter began to work suddenly with
awful force, or at any rate so quickly, that we must call the
motion a whirl: such a whirl as Democritus himself imagined. And since this whirl must be infinitely strong in
order not to be checked through the whole world of the
Infinite weighing heavily upon it, it will be infinitely quick,
for strength can manifest itself originally only in speed. On
the contrary the broader the concentric rings are, the
slower will be this motion; if once the motion could reach
the end of the infinitely extended world, then this motion
would have already infinitely little speed of rotation. Vice
versa, if we conceive of the motion as infinitely great, i.e.,
infinitely quick, at the moment of the very first beginning
of motion, then the original circle must have been infinitely small; we get therefore as the beginning a particle
rotated round itself, a particle with an infinitely small material content. This however would not at all explain the
further motion; one might imagine even all particles of the
primal mass to rotate round themselves and yet the whole
mass would remain unmoved and unseparated. If, however, that material particle of infinite smallness, caught
and swung by the Nous, was not turned round itself but

described a circle somewhat larger than a point, this would cause it to knock against other material particles, to move them on, to hurl them, to make them rebound and thus gradually to stir up a great and spreading tumult within which, as the next result, that separation of the aerial masses from the ethereal had to take place. Just as the commencement of the motion itself is an arbitrary act of the Nous, arbitrary also is the manner of this commencement in so far as the first motion circumscribes a circle of which the radius is chosen somewhat larger than a point.

19

Here of course one might ask, what fancy had at that time so suddenly occurred to the Nous, to knock against some chance material particle out of that number of particles and to turn it around in whirling dance and why that did not occur to It earlier. Whereupon Anaxagoras would answer: "The Nous has the privilege of arbitrary action; It may begin at any chance time, It depends on Itself, whereas everything else is determined from outside. It has no duty, and no end which It might be compelled to pursue; if It did once begin with that motion and set Itself an end, this after all was only—the answer is difficult, Heraclitus would say—play!"

That seems always to have been the last solution or answer hovering on the lips of the Greek. The Anaxagorean Mind is an artist and in truth the most powerful genius of mechanics and architecture, creating with the simplest means the most magnificent forms and tracks and as it were a mobile architecture, but always out of that irrational arbitrariness which lies in the soul of the artist. It is as though Anaxagoras was pointing at Phidias and in face of the immense work of art, the Cosmos, was calling out to us as he would do in front of the Parthenon: "The

Becoming is no moral, but only an artistic phenomenon." Aristotle relates that, to the question what made life worth living, Anaxagoras had answered: "Contemplating the heavens and the total order of the Cosmos." He treated physical things so devotionally, and with that same mysterious awe, which we feel when standing in front of an antique temple; his doctrine became a species of free-thinking religious exercise, protecting itself through the odi profanum vulgus et arceo and choosing its adherents with precaution out of the highest and noblest society of Athens. In the exclusive community of the Athenian Anaxagoreans the mythology of the people was allowed only as a symbolic language; all myths, all gods, all heroes were considered here only as hieroglyphics of the interpretation of nature, and even the Homeric epic was said to be the canonic song of the sway of the Nous and the struggles and laws of Nature. Here and there a note from this society of sublime free-thinkers penetrated to the people; and especially Euripides, the great and at all times daring Euripides, ever thinking of something new, dared to let many things become known by means of the tragic mask, many things which pierced like an arrow through the senses of the masses and from which the latter freed themselves only by means of ludicrous caricatures and ridiculous re-interpretations.

The greatest of all Anaxagoreans however is Pericles, the mightiest and worthiest man of the world; and Plato bears witness that the philosophy of Anaxagoras alone had given that sublime flight to the genius of Pericles. When as a public orator he stood before his people, in the beautiful rigidity and immobility of a marble Olympian and now, calm, wrapped in his mantle, with unruffled drapery, without any change of facial expression, without smile, with a voice the strong tone of which remained ever the same, and when he now spoke in an absolutely un-Demosthenic but merely Periclean fashion, when he thundered, struck with lightnings, annihilated and redeemed—

then he was the epitome of the Anaxagorean Cosmos, the image of the Nous, who has built for Itself the most beautiful and dignified receptacle, then Pericles was as it were the visible human incarnation of the building, moving, eliminating, ordering, reviewing, artistically-undetermined force of the Mind. Anaxagoras himself said man was the most rational being or he must necessarily shelter the Nous within himself in greater fulness than all other beings, because he had such admirable organs as his hands; Anaxagoras concluded therefore, that that Nous, according to the extent to which It made Itself master of a material body, was always forming for Itself out of this material the tools corresponding to Its degree of power, consequently the Nous made the most beautiful and appropriate tools, when It was appearing in his greatest fulness. And as the most wondrous and appropriate action of the Nous was that circular primal-motion, since at that time the Mind was still together, undivided, in Itself, thus to the listening Anaxagoras the effect of the Periclean speech often appeared perhaps as a simile of that circular primal-motion; for here too he perceived a whirl of thoughts moving itself at first with awful force but in an orderly manner, which in concentric circles gradually caught and carried away the nearest and farthest and which, when it reached its end, had reshaped—organizing and segregating—the whole nation.

To the later philosophers of antiquity the way in which Anaxagoras made use of his Nous for the interpretation of the world was strange, indeed scarcely pardonable; to them it seemed as though he had found a grand tool but had not well understood it and they tried to retrieve what the finder had neglected. They therefore did not recognize what meaning the abstention of Anaxagoras, inspired by the purest spirit of the method of natural science, had, and that this abstention first of all in every case puts to itself the question: "What is the cause of Something"? (causa efficiens)—and not "What is the purpose of

Something"? (causa finalis). The Nous has not been dragged in by Anaxagoras for the purpose of answering the special question: "What is the cause of motion and what causes regular motions?"; Plato however reproaches him, that he ought to have, but had not shown that everything was in its own fashion and its own place the most beautiful, the best and the most appropriate. But this Anaxagoras would not have dared to assert in any individual case, to him the existing world was not even the most conceivably perfect world, for he saw everything originate out of everything, and he found the segregation of the substances through the Nous complete and done with, neither at the end of the filled space of the world nor in the individual beings. For his understanding it was sufficient that he had found a motion, which, by simple continued action could create the visible order out of a chaos mixed through and through; and he took good care not to put the question as to the Why? of the motion, as to the rational purpose of motion. For if the Nous had to fulfil by means of motion a purpose innate in the noumenal essence, then it was no longer in Its free will to commence the motion at any chance time; in so far as the Nous is eternal, It had also to be determined eternally by this purpose, and then no point of time could have been allowed to exist in which motion was still lacking, indeed it would have been logically forbidden to assume a starting point for motion: whereby again the conception of original chaos, the basis of the whole Anaxagorean interpretation of the world would likewise have become logically impossible. In order to escape such difficulties, which teleology creates, Anaxagoras had always to emphasize and asseverate that the Mind has free will; all Its actions, including that of the primal motion, were actions of the "free will," whereas on the contrary after that primeval moment the whole remaining world was shaping itself in a strictly determined, and more precisely, mechanically determined form. That absolutely free will however can be conceived only as purposeless, somewhat after the fashion of children's play or the artist's bent for play. It is an error to ascribe to Anaxagoras the common confusion of the teleologist, who, marveling at the extraordinary appropriateness, at the agreement of the parts with the whole, especially in the realm of the organic, assumes that that which exists for the intellect had also come into existence through intellect, and that that which man brings about only under the guidance of the idea of purpose, must have been brought about by Nature through reflection and ideas of purpose. (Schopenhauer, "The World As Will And Idea," vol. ii., Second Book, chap. 26: On Teleology). Conceived in the manner of Anaxagoras, however, the order and appropriateness of things on the contrary is nothing but the immediate result of a blind mechanical motion; and only in order to cause this motion, in order to get for once out of the dead-rest of the Chaos, Anaxagoras assumed the free-willed Nous who depends only on Itself. He appreciated in the Nous just the very quality of being a thing of chance, a chance agent, therefore of being able to act unconditioned, undetermined, guided neither by causes nor by purposes.

NOTES FOR A CONTINUATION

1

That this total conception of the Anaxagorean doctrine must be right, is proved most clearly by the way in which the successors of Anaxagoras, the Agrigentine Empedocles and the atomic teacher Democritus in their counter-systems actually criticized and improved that doctrine. The method of this critique is more than anything a continued renunciation in that spirit of natural science mentioned above, the law of economy applied to the interpretation of nature. That hypothesis, which explains the existing world with the smallest expenditure of assumptions and means is to have preference: for in such a hypothesis is to be found the least amount of arbitrariness, and in it free play with possibilities is prohibited. Should there be two hypotheses which both explain the world, then a strict test must be applied as to which of the two better satisfies that demand of economy. He who can manage this explanation with the simpler and more known forces, especially the mechanical ones, he who deduces the existing edifice of the world out of the smallest possible number of forces, will always be preferred to him who allows the more complicated and less-known forces, and these moreover in greater number, to carry on a world-creating play. So then we see Empedocles endeavoring to remove the superfluity of hypotheses from the doctrine of Anaxagoras.

The first hypothesis which falls as unnecessary is that of the Anaxagorean Nous, for its assumption is much too complex to explain anything so simple as motion. After all it is only necessary to explain the two kinds of motion: the motion of a body towards another, and the motion away from another.

2

If our present Becoming is a segregating, although not a complete one, then Empedocles asks: what prevents complete segregation? Evidently a force works against it, i.e., a latent motion of attraction.

Further: in order to explain that Chaos, a force must already have been at work; a movement is necessary to bring about this complicated entanglement.

Therefore periodical preponderance of the one and the other force is certain. They are opposites.

The force of attraction is still at work; for otherwise there would be no Things at all, everything would be segregated.

This is the actual fact: two kinds of motion. The Nous does not explain them. On the contrary, Love and Hatred; indeed we certainly see that these move as well as that the Nous moves.

Now the conception of the primal state undergoes a change: it is the most blessed. With Anaxagoras it was the chaos before the architectural work, the heap of stones as it were upon the building site.

3

Empedocles had conceived the thought of a tangential force originated by revolution and working against gravity ("de coelo," i., p. 284), Schopenhauer, "W. A. W.," ii. 390.

He considered the continuation of the circular movement according to Anaxagoras impossible. It would result in a whirl, i.e., the contrary of ordered motion.

If the particles were infinitely mixed, pell-mell, then one would be able to break asunder the bodies without any exertion of power, they would not cohere or hold together, they would be as dust.

The forces, which press the atoms against one another, and which give stability to the mass, Empedocles calls "Love." It is a molecular force, a constitutive force of the bodies.

4

Against Anaxagoras.

1. The Chaos already presupposes motion.

2. Nothing prevented the complete segregation.

3. Our bodies would be dust-forms. How can motion exist, if there are not counter-motions in all bodies?

4. An ordered permanent circular motion impossible; only a whirl. He assumes the whirl itself to be an effect of the νεῖκος.—ἀπορροιαί. How do distant things operate on one another, sun upon earth? If everything were still in a whirl, that would be impossible. Therefore at least two moving powers: which must be inherent in Things.

5. Why infinite ὄντα? Transgression of experience. Anaxagoras meant the chemical atoms. Empedocles tried the assumption of four kinds of chemical atoms. He took the aggregate states to be essential, and heat to be coordinated. Therefore the aggregate states through repulsion and attraction; matter in four forms.

6. The periodical principle is necessary.

7. With the living beings Empedocles will also deal still on the same principle. Here also he denies purposiveness. His greatest deed. With Anaxagoras a dualism.

Socrates seeking Alcibiades in the
House of Aspasia (1861)

5

The symbolism of sexual love. Here as in the Platonic fable the longing after Oneness shows itself, and here, likewise, is shown that once a greater unity already existed; were this greater unity established, then this would again strive after a still greater one. The conviction of the unity of everything living guarantees that once there was an immense Living Something, of which we are pieces; that is probably the Sphairos itself. He is the most blessed deity. Everything was connected only through love, therefore in the highest degree appropriate. Love has been torn to pieces and splintered by hatred, love has been divided into her elements and killed—bereft of life. In the whirl no living individuals originate. Eventually everything is segregated and now our period begins. (He opposes the Anaxagorean Primal Mixture by a Primal Discord.) Love, blind as she is, with furious haste again throws the elements one against another endeavoring to see whether she can bring them back to life again or not. Here and there she is successful. It continues. A presentiment originates in the living beings, that they are to strive after still higher unions than home and the primal state. Eros. It is a terrible crime to kill life, for thereby one works back to the Primal Discord. Some day everything will be again one single life, the most blissful state.

The Pythagorean-orphean doctrine re-interpreted in the manner of natural science. Empedocles consciously masters both means of expression, therefore he is the first rhetor. Political aims.

The double-nature—the agonal and the loving, the compassionate.

Attempt of the Hellenic total reform.

All inorganic matter has originated out of organic, it is dead organic matter. Corpse and man.

6

DEMOCRITUS
The greatest possible simplification of the hypotheses.
1. There is motion, therefore vacuum, therefore a "Non-Existent." Thinking is motion.
2. If there is a "Non-Existent" it must be indivisible, i.e., absolutely filled. Division is only explicable in case of empty spaces and pores. The "Non-Existent" alone is an absolutely porous thing.
3. The secondary qualities of matter, νόμῳ, not of Matter-In-Itself.
4. Establishment of the primary qualities of the ἄτομα. Wherein homogeneous, wherein heterogeneous?
5. The aggregate-states of Empedocles (four elements) presuppose only the homogeneous atoms, they themselves cannot therefore be ὄντα.
6. Motion is connected indissolubly with the atoms, effect of gravity. Epicur. Critique: what does gravity signify in an infinite vacuum?
7. Thinking is the motion of the fire-atoms. Soul, life, perceptions of the senses.
. . . .
Value of materialism and its embarrassment.
Plato and Democritus.
The hermit-like homeless noble searcher for truth. Democritus and the Pythagoreans together find the basis of natural sciences.
. . . .
What are the causes which have interrupted a flourishing science of experimental physics in antiquity after Democritus?

7

Anaxagoras has taken from Heraclitus the idea that in every Becoming and in every Being the opposites are together.

He felt strongly the contradiction that a body has many qualities and he pulverized it in the belief that he had now dissolved it into its true qualities.

. . . .

Plato: first Heraclitean, later Sceptic: Everything, even Thinking, is in a state of flux.

Brought through Socrates to the permanence of the good, the beautiful.

These assumed as entitative.

All generic ideals partake of the idea of the good, the beautiful, and they too are therefore entitative, being (as the soul partakes of the idea of Life). The idea is formless.

Through Pythagoras' metempsychosis has been answered the question: how we can know anything about the ideas.

Plato's end: skepticism in Parmenides. Refutation of ideology.

8

CONCLUSION

Greek thought during the tragic age is pessimistic or artistically optimistic.

Their judgment about life implies more.

The One, flight from the Becoming. Aut unity, aut artistic play.

Deep distrust of reality: nobody assumes a good god, who has made everything optime.

{Pythagoreans, religious sect.

{Anaximander.
{Empedocles.
Eleates.
{Anaxagoras.
{Heraclitus.
Democritus: the world without moral and aesthetic meaning, pessimism of chance.

. . . .

If one placed a tragedy before all these, the three former would see in it the mirror of the fatality of existence, Parmenides a transitory appearance, Heraclitus and Anaxagoras an artistic edifice and image of the world-laws, Democritus the result of machines.

. . . .

With Socrates Optimism begins, an optimism no longer artistic, with teleology and faith in the good god; faith in the enlightened good man. Dissolution of the instincts, Socrates breaks with the hitherto prevailing knowledge and culture; he intends returning to the old citizen-virtue and to the State.

Plato dissociates himself from the State, when he observes that the State has become identical with the new Culture.

The Socratic skepticism is a weapon against the hitherto prevailing culture and knowledge.

The crowd salutes the return of Alcibiades.

ON TRUTH AND FALSITY IN THEIR ULTRAMORAL SENSE

1.

In some remote corner of the universe, effused into innumerable solar-systems, there was once a star upon which clever animals invented cognition. It was the haughtiest, most mendacious moment in the history of this world, but yet only a moment. After Nature had taken breath awhile the star congealed and the clever animals had to die.—Someone might write a fable after this style, and yet he would not have illustrated sufficiently, how wretched,; shadow-like, transitory, purposeless and fanciful the human intellect appears in Nature. There were eternities during which this intellect did not exist, and when it has once more passed away there will be nothing to show that it has existed. For this intellect is not concerned with any further mission transcending the sphere of human life. No, it is purely human and none but its owner and procreator regards it so pathetically as to suppose that the world revolves around it. If, however, we and the gnat could understand each other we should learn that even the gnat swims through the air with the same pathos, and feels within itself the flying center of the world. Nothing in Nature is so bad or so insignificant that it will not, at the smallest puff of that force cognition, immediately swell up like a balloon, and just as a mere porter wants to have his admirer, so the very proudest man, the philosopher, imagines he sees from all sides the eyes of the universe telescopically directed upon his actions and thoughts.

It is remarkable that this is accomplished by the intellect, which after all has been given to the most unfortunate, the most delicate, the most transient beings only as an expedient, in order to detain them for a moment in existence, from which without that extra-gift they would have every cause to flee as swiftly as Lessing's son.[1] That haughtiness connected with cognition and sensation, spreading blinding fogs before the eyes and over the senses of men, deceives itself therefore as to the value of existence owing to the fact that it bears within itself the most flattering evaluation of cognition. Its most general effect is deception; but even its most particular effects have something of deception in their nature.

The intellect, as a means for the preservation of the individual, develops its chief power in dissimulation; for it is by dissimulation that the feebler, and less robust individuals preserve themselves, since it has been denied them to fight the battle of existence with horns or the sharp teeth of beasts of prey. In man this art of dissimulation reaches its acme of perfection: in him deception, flattery, falsehood and fraud, slander, display, pretentiousness, disguise, cloaking convention, and acting to others and to himself in short, the continual fluttering to and fro around the one flame—Vanity: all these things are so much the rule, and the law, that few things are more incomprehensible than the way in which an honest and pure impulse to truth could have arisen among men. They are deeply immersed in illusions and dream-fancies; their eyes glance only over the surface of things and see "forms"; their sensation nowhere leads to truth, but contents itself with receiving stimuli and, so to say, with playing hide-and-seek on the back of things. In addition to that, at night man allows his dreams to lie to him a whole life-time long, without his moral sense ever trying to prevent them; whereas men are said to exist who by the exercise of a strong will have overcome the habit of snoring. What indeed does man know about himself? Oh! that he could but once see himself complete, placed as it were in an illuminated glass-case! Does not nature keep secret from him most things, even about his body, e.g., the convolutions of the intestines, the quick flow of the blood-currents, the intricate vibrations of the fibers, so as to banish and lock him up in proud, delusive knowledge? Nature threw away the key; and woe co the fateful curiosity which might be able for a moment to look out and down through a crevice in the chamber of consciousness, and discover that man, indifferent to his own ignorance, is resting on the pitiless, the greedy, the insatiable, the murderous, and, as it were, hanging in dreams on the back of a tiger. Whence, in the wide world, with this state of affairs, arises the impulse to truth?

As far as the individual tries to preserve himself against other individuals, in the natural state of things he uses the intellect in most cases only for dissimulation; since, however, man both from necessity and boredom wants to exist socially and gregariously, he must needs make peace and at least endeavor to cause the greatest bellum omnium contra omnes to disappear from his world. This first conclusion of peace brings with it a something which looks like the first step towards the attainment of that enigmatical bent for truth. For that which henceforth is to be "truth" is now fixed; that is to say, a uniformly valid and binding designation of things is invented and the legislature of language also gives the first laws of truth: since here, for the first time, originates the contrast between truth and falsity. The liar uses the valid designations, the words, in order to make the unreal appear as real; e.g., he says, "I am rich," whereas the right designation for his state would be "poor." He abuses the fixed conventions by convenient substitution or even inversion of terms. If he does this in a selfish and moreover harmful fashion, society will no longer trust him but will even exclude him. In this way men avoid not so much being defrauded, but being injured by fraud. At bottom, at this juncture too, they hate not deception, but the evil, hostile consequences of certain species of deception. And it is in a similarly limited sense only that man desires truth: he covets the agreeable, life-preserving

consequences of truth; he is indifferent towards pure, ineffective knowledge; he is even inimical towards truths
which possibly might prove harmful or destroying. And,
moreover, what after all are those conventions op language? Are they possibly products of knowledge, of the
love of truth; do the designations and the things coincide?
Is language the adequate expression of all realities?

Only by means of forgetfulness can man ever arrive at
imagining that he possesses "truth" in that degree just indicated. If he does not mean to content himself with truth
in the shape of tautology, that is, with empty husks, he
will always obtain illusions instead of truth. What is a
word? The expression of a nerve-stimulus in sounds. But
to infer a cause outside us from the nerve-stimulus is already the result of a wrong and unjustifiable application
of the proposition of causality. How should we dare, if
truth with the genesis of language, if the point of view of
certainty with the designations had alone been decisive;
how indeed should we dare to say: the stone is hard; as if
"hard" was known to us otherwise; and not merely as an
entirely subjective stimulus! We divide things according to
genders; we designate the tree as masculine,[2] the plant
as feminine:[3] what arbitrary metaphors! How far flown
beyond the canon of certainty! We speak of a "serpent";[4]
the designation fits nothing but the sinuosity, and could
therefore also appertain to the worm. What arbitrary de-
marcations! what one-sided preferences given sometimes
to this, sometimes to that quality of a thing! The different
languages placed side by side show that with words truth
or adequate expression matters little: for otherwise there
would not be so many languages. The "Thing-in-itself" (it
is just this which would be the pure ineffective truth) is
also quite incomprehensible to the creator of language and
not worth making any great endeavor to obtain. He designates only the relations of things to men and for their
expression he calls to his help the most daring metaphors.
A nerve-stimulus, first transformed into a percept! First

metaphor! The percept again copied into a sound! Second metaphor! And each time he leaps completely out of one sphere right into the midst of an entirely different one. One can imagine a man who is quite deaf and has never had a sensation of tone and of music; just as this man will possibly marvel at Chladni's sound figures in the sand, will discover their cause in the vibrations of the string, and will then proclaim that now he knows what man calls "tone"; even so does it happen to us all with language. When we talk about trees, colors, snow and flowers, we believe we know something about the things themselves, and yet we only possess metaphors of the things, and these metaphors do not in the least correspond to the original essentials. Just as the sound shows itself as a sand-figure, in the same way the enigmatical x of the Thing-in-itself is seen first as nerve-stimulus, then as percept, and finally as sound. At any rate the genesis of language did not therefore proceed on logical lines, and the whole material in which and with which the man of truth, the investigator, the philosopher works and builds, originates, if not from Nephelococcygia, cloud-land, at any rate not from the essence of things.

Let us especially think about the formation of ideas. Every word becomes at once an idea not by having, as one might presume, to serve as a reminder for the original experience happening but once and absolutely individualized, to which experience such word owes its origin, no, but by having simultaneously to fit innumerable, more or less similar (which really means never equal, therefore altogether unequal) cases. Every idea originates through equating the unequal. As certainly as no one leaf is exactly similar to any other, so certain is it that the idea "leaf" has been formed through an arbitrary omission of these individual differences, through a forgetting of the differentiating qualities, and this idea now awakens the notion that in nature there is, besides the leaves, a something called the "leaf," perhaps a primal form according to which all leaves were woven, drawn, accurately measured, colored, crinkled, painted, but by unskilled hands, so that no copy had turned out correct and trustworthy as a true copy of the primal form. We call a man "honest"; we ask, why has he acted so honestly to-day? Our customary answer runs, "On account of his honesty." The Honesty! That means again: the "leaf" is the cause of the leaves. We really and truly do not know anything at all about an essential quality which might be called the honesty, but we do know about numerous individualized, and therefore unequal actions, which we equate by omission of the unequal, and now designate as honest actions; finally out of them we formulate a qualitas occulta with the name "Honesty." The disregarding of the individual and real furnishes us with the idea, as it likewise also gives us the form; whereas nature knows of no forms and ideas, and therefore knows no species but only an x, to us inaccessible and indefinable. For our antithesis of individual and species is anthropomorphic too and does not come from the essence of things, although on the other hand we do not dare to say that it does not correspond to it; for that would be a dogmatic assertion and as such just as indemonstrable as its contrary.

What therefore is truth? A mobile army of metaphors, metonymies, anthropomorphisms: in short a sum of human relations which became poetically and rhetorically intensified, metamorphosed, adorned, and after long usage seem to a nation fixed, canonic and binding; truths are illusions of which one has forgotten that they are illusions; worn-out metaphors which have become powerless to affect the senses; coins which have their obverse effaced and now are no longer of account as coins but merely as metal.

Still we do not yet know whence the impulse to truth comes, for up to now we have heard only about the obligation which society imposes in order to exist: to be truthful, that is, to use the usual metaphors, therefore

expressed morally: we have heard only about the obligation to lie according to a fixed convention, to lie
gregariously in a style binding for all. Now man of course
forgets that matters are going thus with him; he therefore
lies in that fashion pointed out unconsciously and according to habits of centuries' standing—and by this very
unconsciousness, by this very forgetting, he arrives at a
sense for truth. Through this feeling of being obliged to
designate one thing as "red," another as "cold," a third one
as "dumb," awakes a moral emotion relating to truth. Out
of the antithesis "liar" whom nobody trusts, whom all exclude, man demonstrates to himself the venerableness,
reliability, usefulness of truth. Now as a "rational" being
he submits his actions to the sway of abstractions; he no
longer suffers himself to be carried away by sudden impressions, by sensations, he first generalizes all these
impressions into paler, cooler ideas, in order to attach to
them the ship of his life and actions. Everything which
makes man stand out in bold relief against the animal depends on this faculty of volatilizing the concrete
metaphors into a schema, and therefore resolving a perception into an idea. For within the range of those
schemata a something becomes possible that never could
succeed under the first perceptual impressions: to build
up a pyramidal order with castes and grades, to create a
new world of laws, privileges, sub-orders, delimitations,
which now stands opposite the other perceptual world of
first impressions and assumes the appearance of being the
more fixed, general, known, human of the two and therefore the regulating and imperative one. Whereas every
metaphor of perception is individual and without its equal
and therefore knows how to escape all attempts to classify
it, the great "edifice of ideas shows the rigid regularity of a
Roman Columbarium and in logic breathes forth the
sternness and coolness which we find in mathematics. He
who has been breathed upon by this coolness will scarcely
believe, that the idea too, bony and hexa-hedral, and

permutable as a die, remains however only as the residuum of a metaphor, and that the illusion of the artistic metamorphosis of a nerve-stimulus into percepts is, if not the mother, then the grand-mother of every idea. Now in this game of dice, "Truth" means to use every die as it is designated, to count its points carefully, to form exact classifications, and never lo violate the order of castes and the sequences of rank. Just as the Romans and Etruscans for their benefit cut up the sky by means of strong mathematical lines and banned a god as it were into a templum, into a space limited in this fashion, so every nation has above its head such a sky of ideas divided up mathematically, and it understands the demand for truth to mean that every conceptual god is to be looked for only in his own sphere. One may here well admire man, who succeeded in piling up an infinitely complex dome of ideas on a movable foundation and as it were on running water, as a powerful genius of architecture. Of course in order to obtain hold on such a foundation it must be as an edifice piled up out of cobwebs, so fragile, as to be carried away by the waves: so firm, as not to be blown asunder by every wind. In this way man as an architectural genius rises high above the bee; she builds with wax, which she brings together out of nature; he with the much more delicate material of ideas, which he must first manufacture within himself. He is very much to be admired here—but not on account of his impulse for truth, his bent for pure cognition of things. If somebody hides a thing behind a bush, seeks it again and finds it in the self-same place, then there is not much to boast of, respecting this seeking and finding; thus, however, matters stand with the seeking and finding of "truth" within the realm of reason. If I make the definition of the mammal and then declare after inspecting a camel, "Behold a mammal," then no doubt a truth is brought to light thereby, but it is of very limited value, I mean it is anthropomorphic through and through, and does not contain one single point which is "true-in-itself," real and universally valid, apart from man. The seeker after such truths seeks at the bottom only the metamorphosis of the world in man, he strives for an understanding of the world as a human-like thing and by his battling gains at best the feeling of an assimilation. Similarly, as the astrologer contemplated the stars in the service of man and in connection with their happiness and unhappiness, such a seeker contemplates the whole world as related to man, as the infinitely protracted echo of an original sound: man; as the multiplied copy of the one arch-type: man. His procedure is to apply man as the measure of all things, whereby he starts from the error of believing that he has these things immediately before him as pure objects. He therefore forgets that the original metaphors of perception are metaphors, and takes them for the things themselves.

Only by forgetting that primitive world of metaphors, only by the congelation and coagulation of an original mass of similes and percepts pouring forth as a fiery liquid out of the primal faculty of human fancy, only by the invincible faith, that this sun, this window, this table is a truth in itself: in short only by the fact that man forgets himself as subject, and what is more as an artistically creating subject: only by all this does he live with some repose, safety and consequence. If he were able to get out of the prison walls of this faith, even for an instant only, his "self-consciousness would be destroyed at once. Already it costs him some trouble to admit to himself that the insect and the bird perceive a world different from his own, and that the question, which of the two world-perceptions is more accurate, is quite a senseless one, since to decide this question it would be necessary to apply the standard of right perception, i.e., to apply a standard which does not exist. On the whole it seems to me that the "right perception"—which would mean the adequate expression of an object in the subject—is a nonentity full of contradictions: for between two utterly different spheres, as between subject and object, there is no causality, no accuracy, no expression, but at the utmost an aesthetical relation, I mean a suggestive metamorphosis, a stammering translation into quite a distinct foreign language, for which purpose however there is needed at any rate an intermediate sphere, an intermediate force, freely composing and freely inventing. The word "phenomenon" contains many seductions, and on that account I avoid it as much as possible, for it is not true that the essence of things appears in the empiric world. A painter who had no hands and wanted to express the picture distinctly present to his mind by the agency of song, would still reveal much more with this permutation of spheres, than the empiric world reveals about the essence of things. The very relation of a nerve-stimulus to the produced percept is in itself no necessary one; but if the same percept has been reproduced millions of times and has been the inheritance of many successive generations of man, and in the end appears each time to all mankind as the result of the same cause, then it attains finally for man the same importance as if it were the unique, necessary percept and as if that relation between the original nerve-stimulus and the percept produced were a close relation of causality: just as a dream eternally repeated, would be perceived and judged as though real. But the congelation and coagulation of a metaphor does not at all guarantee the necessity and exclusive justification of that metaphor.

Surely every human being who is at home with such contemplations has felt a deep distrust against any idealism of that kind, as often as he has distinctly convinced himself of the eternal rigidity, omni-presence, and infallibility of nature's laws: he has arrived at the conclusion that as far as we can penetrate the heights of the telescopic and the depths of the microscopic world, everything is quite secure, complete, infinite, determined, and continuous. Science will have to dig in these shafts eternally and successfully and all things found are sure to have to harmonize and not to contradict one another. How little does this resemble a product of fancy, for if it were one it would necessarily betray somewhere its nature of appearance and unreality. Against this it may be objected in the first place that if each of us had for himself a different sensibility, if we ourselves were only able to perceive sometimes as a bird, sometimes as a worm, sometimes as a plant, or if one of us saw the same stimulus as red, another as blue, if a third person even perceived it as a tone, then nobody would talk of such an orderliness of nature, but would conceive of her only as an extremely subjective structure. Secondly, what is, for us in general, a law of nature? It is not known in itself but only in its effects, that is to say in its relations to other laws of nature, which again are known to us only as sums of relations. Therefore all these relations refer only one to another and are absolutely incomprehensible to us in their essence; only that which we add: time, space, i.e., relations of sequence and numbers, are really known to us in them. Everything wonderful, however, that we marvel at in the laws of nature, everything that demands an explanation and might seduce us into distrusting idealism, lies really and solely in the mathematical rigor and inviolability of the conceptions of time and space. These however we produce within ourselves and throw them forth with that necessity with which the spider spins; since we are compelled to conceive all things under these forms only, then it is no longer wonderful that in all things we actually conceive none but these forms: for they all must bear within themselves the laws of number, and this very idea of number is the most marvelous in all things. All obedience to law which impresses us so forcibly in the orbits of stars and in chemical processes coincides at the bottom with those qualities which we ourselves attach to those things, so that it is we who thereby make the impression upon ourselves. Whence it clearly follows that that artistic formation of metaphors, with which every sensation in us begins, already presupposes those forms, and is therefore only consummated within them; only out of the persistency of these primal forms the possibility explains itself, how afterwards—out of the metaphors themselves a structure of ideas, could again be compiled. For the latter is an imitation of the relations of time, space and number in the realm of metaphors.

[1] The German poet, Lessing, had been married for just a little over one year to Eva König. A son was born and died the same day, and the mother's life was despaired of. In a letter to his friend Eschenburg the poet wrote: "... and I lost him so unwillingly, this son! For he had so much understanding! so much understanding! Do not suppose that the few hours of fatherhood have made me an ape of a father! I know what I say. Was it not understanding, that they had to drag him into the world with a pair of forceps? that he so soon suspected the evil of this world? Was it not understanding, that he seized the first opportunity to get away from it?..."

Eva König died a week later.—TR.

[2] In German the tree—der Baum—is masculine.—TR.

[3] In German the plant—die Pflanze—-is feminine—TR.

[4] Cf. the German die Schlange and schlingen, the English serpent from the Latin serpere.—TR.

2

As we saw, it is language which has worked originally at the construction of ideas; in later times it is science.

Just as the bee works at the same time at the cells and fills them with honey, thus science works irresistibly at that great columbarium of ideas, the cemetery of perceptions, builds ever newer and higher storeys; supports, purifies, renews the old cells, and endeavors above all to fill that gigantic framework and to arrange within it the whole of the empiric world, i.e., the anthropomorphic world. And as the man of action binds his life to reason and its ideas, in order to avoid being swept away and losing himself, so the seeker after truth builds his hut close to the towering edifice of science in order to collaborate with it and to find protection. And he needs protection. For there are awful powers which continually press upon him, and which hold out against the "truth" of science "truths" fashioned in quite another way, bearing devices of the most heterogeneous character.

That impulse towards the formation of metaphors, mat fundamental impulse of man, which we cannot reason away for one moment—for thereby we should reason away man himself—is in truth not defeated nor even subdued by the fact that out of its evaporated products, the ideas, a regular and rigid new world has been built as a stronghold for it. This impulse seeks for itself a new realm of action and another river-bed, and finds it in Mythos and more generally in Art. This impulse constantly confuses the rubrics and cells of the ideas, by putting up new figures of speech, metaphors, metonymies; it constantly shows its passionate longing for shaping the existing world of waking man as motley, irregular, inconsequentially incoherent, attractive, and eternally new as the world of dreams is. For indeed, waking man per se is only clear about his being awake through the rigid and orderly woof of ideas, and it is for this very reason that he sometimes comes to believe that he was dreaming when that woof of ideas has for a moment been torn by Art. Pascal is quite right, when he asserts, that if the same dream came to us every night we should be just as much occupied by it as by the things which we see every day; to quote his words, "If an artisan were certain that he would dream every night for fully twelve hours that he was a king, I believe that he would be just as happy as a king who dreams every night for twelve hours that he is an artisan." The wide-awake day of a people mystically excitable, let us say of the earlier Greeks, is in fact through the continually-working wonder, which the mythos presupposes, more akin to the dream than to the day of the thinker sobered by science. If every tree may at some time talk as a nymph, or a god under the disguise of a bull, carry away virgins, if the goddess Athene herself be suddenly seen as, with a beautiful team, she drives, accompanied by Pisistratus, through the markets of Athens—and every honest Athenian did believe this—at any moment, as in a dream, everything is possible; and all nature swarms around man as if she were nothing but the masquerade of the gods, who found it a huge joke to deceive man by assuming all possible forms.

Man himself, however, has an invincible tendency to let himself be deceived, and he is like one enchanted with happiness when the rhapsodist narrates to him epic romances in such a way that they appear real or when the actor on the stage makes the king appear more kingly than reality shows him. Intellect, that master of dissimulation, is free and dismissed from his service as slave, so long as It is able to deceive without injuring, and then It celebrates Its Saturnalia. Never is It richer, prouder, more luxuriant, more skillful and daring; with a creator's delight It throws metaphors into confusion, shifts the boundary-stones of the abstractions, so that for instance It designates the stream as the mobile way which carries man to that place whither he would otherwise go. Now It has thrown off Its shoulders the emblem of servitude. Usually with gloomy officiousness It endeavors to point out the way to a poor individual coveting existence, and It fares forth for plunder and booty like a servant for his master, but now It Itself has become a master and may wipe from Its countenance the expression of indigence. Whatever It now does, compared with Its former doings, bears within itself dissimulation, just as Its former doings bore the character of distortion. It copies human life, but takes it for a good thing and seems to rest quite satisfied with it. That enormous framework and hoarding of ideas, by clinging to which needy man saves himself through life, is to the freed intellect only a scaffolding and a toy for Its most daring feats, and when It smashes it to pieces, throws it into confusion, and then puts it together ironically, pairing the strangest, separating the nearest items, then It manifests that It has no use for those makeshifts of misery, and that It is now no longer led by ideas but by intuitions. From these intuitions no regular road leads into the land of the spectral schemata, the abstractions; for them the word is not made, when man sees them he is dumb, or speaks in forbidden metaphors and in unheard-of combinations of ideas, in order to correspond creatively with the impression of the powerful present intuition at least by destroying and jeering at the old barriers of ideas.

There are ages, when the rational and the intuitive man stand side by side, the one full of fear of the intuition, the other full of scorn for the abstraction; the latter just as irrational as the former is inartistic. Both desire to rule over life; the one by knowing how to meet the most important needs with foresight, prudence, regularity; the other as an "over-joyous" hero by ignoring those needs and taking that life only as real which simulates appearance and beauty. Wherever intuitive man, as for instance in the earlier history of Greece, brandishes his weapons more powerfully and victoriously than his opponent, there under favorable conditions, a culture can develop and art can establish her rule over life. That dissembling, that denying of neediness, that splendor of metaphorical notions and especially that directness of dissimulation accompany all utterances of such a life. Neither the house of man, nor his way of walking, nor his clothing, nor his earthen jug suggest that necessity invented them; it seems as if they all were intended as the expressions of a sublime happiness, an Olympic cloudlessness, and as it were a playing at seriousness. Whereas the man guided by ideas and abstractions only wards off misfortune by means of them, without even enforcing for himself happiness out of the abstractions; whereas he strives after the greatest possible freedom from pains, the intuitive man dwelling in the midst of culture has from his intuitions a harvest: besides the warding off of evil, he attains a continuous in-pouring of enlightenment, enlivenment and redemption. Of course when he does suffer, he suffers more: and he even suffers more frequently since he cannot learn from experience, but again and again falls into the same ditch into which he has fallen before. In suffering he is just as irrational as in happiness; he cries aloud and finds no consolation. How different matters are in the same misfortune with the Stoic, taught by experience and ruling himself by ideas! He who otherwise only looks for uprightness, truth, freedom from deceptions and shelter from ensnaring and sudden attack, in his misfortune performs the masterpiece of dissimulation, just as the other did in his happiness; he shows no twitching mobile human face but as it were a mask with dignified, harmonious features; he does not cry out and does not even alter his voice; when a heavy thundercloud bursts upon him, he wraps himself up in his cloak and with slow and measured step walks away from beneath it.

THE END

The Acropolis and Areios Pagos in Athens
by Leo von Klenze (1846)

Made in the USA
Monee, IL
13 May 2023

1308b319-3148-49fa-9326-b16c047daa80R01